Sacro-Egoism

Sacro-Egoism

The Rise of Religious Individualism in the West

John S. Knox

FOREWORD BY
Terry Steele

AFTERWORD BY
Bill Pubols

WIPF & STOCK · Eugene, Oregon

SACRO-EGOISM
The Rise of Religious Individualism in the West

Wipf & Stock
An Imprint of Wipf and Stock Publishers
199 W. 8th Ave., Suite 3
Eugene, OR 97401

www.wipfandstock.com

PAPERBACK ISBN: 978-1-4982-0008-0
HARDCOVER ISBN: 978-1-4982-8689-3

Manufactured in the U.S.A.

For My Dad.

Contents

Illustrations

Foreword

THE WORLD IS CHANGING before our eyes with ethic shifts across national boundaries, economic struggles, and the rise of the Emerging culture in the face of Modernism's decline. As these and other changes take place, religion and spirituality in the West are also being affected. For decades, Social Scientists have sharply debated the trends of spirituality and religion in North America. One prevaling theme amongst many scholars is a belief that secularization is gaining strength and that the influence of religion is diminishing. Another theory points to trends of accomodation and spiritual revitalization shown in the development of post-Christendom churches, the progress of the House Church movement, and the growth of the Emerging Church movement. Still others believe that the rising tide of designer religions, American folk religions, and the influence of individualism on spirituality point to the possibility of transformation.

John S. Knox examines these theories in relation to the attitudes and practices of a small town in Oregon. The McMinville Project, undertaken as a comparison study from the Kendal Project in the UK, looks at current trends that reinforce or challenge religious and sociological theories described in Knox's *Sacro-Egoism: The Rise of Religious Individualism in the West*.

Knox examines the sources of spiritual authority in the lives of citizens in the Northwest town of McMinville, Oregon. He seeks answers through a series of qualitative and quantitative devices, mirroring the similar study in the UK. This comparitive study is important for religious practicitioners in discovering the prevailing paths of spiritual growth in the Pacific Northwest and how the local church could adapt or react to these trends.

The Pacific Northwest is often described by locals as a spiritual widerness; The I-5 corridor from Belingham, Washington to Eugene, Oregon, often referred to as "the dark corridor," has long struggled with developing and maintaining a religious identity. Stability of churches in the region has historically been in flux, waxing and waning, but never quite establishing strong enough roots to exert lasting spiritual or social influence. Having one of the highest rates of individualism in the United States, organized religion in the Pacific Northwest has consistently struggled with corporate identity and spiritual growth. In the face of a wide variety of religious options and expectation to explore one's own spirituality, Northwest opinion polls have continuously shown some of the lowest religious identification percentages in the US. A large percentage of people in the Northwest who identify with no religious tradition have been called "the Nones."

While the Pacific Northwest ranks high amongst the Nones, it is not necessarily lacking in spirituality. Non-traditional religious centers are found throughout the region's cities and rural areas. Spiritual Renewal Centers, Celtic Druid worship groups, and various forms of Westernized Buddhism and Hinduism litter urban and rural areas of the Pacific Northwest.

In terms of migration trends, the Pacific Northwest has become one of the nation's largest magnets of the Emerging culture (formerly called Generation X and Millennials). As Modernity is being challenged, members of the Emerging culture are seeking religious practices that embody the ideals of their culture. There seems to be a marked rejection of many theologies and religious trappings associated with Modern religions, especially those within the established Christian church. Key cultural indicators (such as the growth of "enlightened" mysticism and dissatisfaction with rational answers) imply a fundamental shift in culture, altering the dominant paradigm away from Modernity toward Postmodernity.

The Pacific Northwest has been host to experimental religious activities, religious social justice, and experiential worship practices. Foremost amongst the Emerging church's complaints is the modern church's embrace of Enlightenment characteristics, especially the elevation of rational thought, dominance of science, individualism, mechanism, and rampant categorization, including the separation between natural and supernatural realms.

These struggles and trends lead to complex issues pertaining to spiritual journeys of Pacific Northwesterners and more questions for religion on a national scale. How do those in the Pacific Northwest percieve organized religion? Do these trends mirror larger trends? What do these trends signify for the future of Western religion? How should Christian churches respond to these changes?

Knox chose McMinville, Oregon as a kind of control group to test current theories and trends to show whether religion is growing, shrinking or changing and why. Because of its unique and yet representative history, Oregon offers perhaps a microcosmic sample of a larger trend in Western religious thought and practice. Due to its never having had a state religion and being one of the least churched regions in the US, the Pacific Northwest offers a great example of Sacro-Egoism expressed in attitudes and action in its individuals and communities.

Knox raises questions about the state of religion and spirituality in the West that are relevant to these major cultural changes. He outlines the current debate about spirituality in the US, focusing on three possible outcomes: spiritual revitilization, growing secularism, and individualized designer religion. His survey of relevant literature surrounding Congregational Studies and the Sociology of Religion presents a collage of current thinkers' salient points about the issues of faith, growth, social trends and cultural direction for spirituality in the Northwest. Knox's concern for current issues that impact spiritual belief and the

Christian church is clearly demonstrated in his research and writing on issues that are especially important to the dark corridor of the Pacific Northwest and the future of faith in the West.

Terry Steele

PhD in Intercultural Studies
Doctor of Missiology
Professor, George Fox University

Acknowledgments

FIRST AND FOREMOST, I offer my sincerest gratitude to my supervisor, Dr. Ben Pink Dandelion, who has supported me throughout my PhD program with his amazing knowledge, skills, encouragement, flexibility, and compassion. I could not have wished for a better supervisor in the study of the Sociology of Religion. Did I mention how patient he was?

Next, I offer my heart-felt gratitude to the students who assisted me with the demographic count in McMinnville on "Super Sunday" and during the Street Survey. They allowed me to collect a plethora of data without too much stress and anguish. Their positive, mature attitudes deserve the highest acclamation and praise.

I would also like to thank the company of scholars who gave me valuable feedback regarding my sociological hypothesis at the SSSR, ASR, BSA, and Denton conferences over the years. Your kind, erudite remarks and dialogues helped me better define and express my theory. I look forward to more interaction in the future on this exciting topic.

Additionally, I appreciate the editorial and proofing assistance during the final stages of writing by my brother, George; comrade and Oxford graduate, Steve; and racquetball partner and Nampa pastor, Keith. You all helped me improve upon my work while still allowing it to be mine.

Furthermore, I am also deeply indebted to both Dr. Terry Steele and BSC Director Bill Pubols for graciously and expertly contributing the foreword and afterword, respectively. It has been a joy and privilege to dialogue with you both about the present and future state of religiosity in the West. Not only do you both know your stuff, but you are very generous in sharing it with me, thankfully.

Of course, I would not have been able to complete this book without the on-going support and love of my wife, Brenda, and my very patient sons, Jacob and Joe. They graciously gave me time to be away in England to research, and time in Oregon and Idaho to write, and did so with a cheerful and sacrificial heart. I am not sure if they are Sacro-Egoists or Sacro-Communalists, but I love them more than one paragraph can impart.

Last, I am so thankful to God for allowing me to be used in his service. They may not be the tallest mountains, but you still raise me up and provide the most amazing vistas in my life. I never would have dreamed that my life could be so good when I began my studies decades ago.

1

The Sociological Context of the West and the Sacro-States

1.0 Introduction

IN THE WESTERN WORLD today, it is not difficult to find a multitude of articles, books, and television reports (either scholarly and popular) discussing the future and nature of religion in contemporary modern culture. In 2008, a Gallup poll in America indicated, "Two-thirds of Americans think religion is losing its influence on US life, a sharp jump from just three years ago when Americans were nearly evenly split in the question."[1] That same year, a Baylor University survey in 2008 suggested, "American religion is remarkably stable and quite surprising in its diverse beliefs, practices and realities."[2] As Charles Taylor remarked, "For those who see secularism as part of modernity, and modernity as fundamentally progress, the last few decades have been painful and bewildering."[3] What seemed so clearly to point toward the final chapter of church

1. Saad, "Americans Believe Religion is Losing Clout;" online: http://www.gallup.com/poll/113533/Americans-Believe-Religion-Losing-Clout.aspx.

2. Fogleman, "Baylor Survey Finds New Perspectives On U.S. Religious Landscape;" online: http://www.baylor.edu/pr/news.php?action=story&story=52815#.

3. Taylor, "Religious Mobilizations," 281.

life in the West is becoming less likely, especially considering what Americans are saying about the importance of their religious and spiritual lives.

By no means an exceptional American advent, religious life in Europe is also changing, but not necessarily toward morbidity, according to scholars like Nigel Aston who states,

> Church organizations have moved to the margins, and the religious and political elites have long ceased to be interchangeable. Nevertheless, alongside the undoubted political shrinkage, the Churches continue to be social institutions deeply rooted in—and usually responsive to—community life and possessed of diverse cultural appeal.[4]

Sources such as these provide a plethora of opinions on the waxing and waning of religion in Europe and America based on various trends or patterns observable in the religious and spiritual communities once assumed by some earlier scholars and theologians to be an immutable presence in western society. However, the aforementioned sociological studies in both Europe and America along with demographical data from sources such as the Pew Research Center,[5] Kendal Project,[6] the ARIS study,[7] and the Baylor study,[8] seem to suggest otherwise.

4. Aston, "Decline or Evolution? Religion in Modern Europe," 99.

5. "America's Changing Religious Landscape: Christians Decline Sharply as Share of Population; Unaffiliated and Other Faiths Continue to Grow;" online: http://www.pewforum.org/2015/05/12/americas-changing-religious-landscape/.

6. *The Kendal Project*; online: http://www.lancs.ac.uk/fss/projects/ieppp/kendal/.

7. "American Religious Identification Survey 2001;" online: http://www.gc.cuny.edu/faculty/research_briefs/aris/aris_part_two.htm.

8. "American Piety in the 21st Century;" online: http://www.baylor.edu/isreligion/index.php?id=40634.

1.1 The Sociological Context

So, what is actually going on, religiously, in the West? Certainly, spiritual expressions are transforming, but their present (and future) condition is the focus of much heated debate. Questions abound about whether religious life is waning, transforming, or reinvigorating traditional avenues in modern society. From the sociological side, some claim the current religious milieu is the result of a flooded religious market;[9] others claim (or have claimed) it is due to the secularization of modern culture.[10]

Sociologists like Steve Bruce suggest that with the secularization and modernization of the West comes a growing uselessness and irrelevance of religion in greater society. In his opinion, there are "irreversible" trends and thus, the importance of religion and Christianity will wane in several places where it used to reign. Thus, the current spirituality and religiosity in the West is just " . . . the last gasp and whimper of concern with the sacred in the West, an inconsequential dabbling that is doomed to disappear almost as quickly as it appeared."[11]

Countering this, rational choice theorists Finke and Stark suggest that religion in America has always been about a religious market-driven economy—the churches that offer the most emotionally and spiritually have statistically come out on top. These scholars do not see religion and Christianity as weakening; rather, they simply see modern society desiring new religious markets into which to put their religious faith. Secularization does occur, but instead of putting mortal pressure upon religious entities, secularization forces established churches and denominations to become more marketable to the public.[12]

9. Finke and Stark, *Churching of America, 1776–1990*; Iannaccone and Everton, "Never on Sunny Days: Lessons From Weekly Attendance Counts."

10 Wilson, "Prediction and Prophecy in the Future of Religion," 64–73; Berger, *The Social Reality of Religion*; Bruce, *God is Dead*.

11. Heelas et al., *The Spiritual Revolution* 2.

12. Finke and Stark, *The Churching of America*, 271–272.

Churches are adjusting to the new, modern religious scene in order to flourish or even survive. Every major city in America has its own megachurch. Thus, "The result is not a decline in religion, but only a decline in the fortunes of specific religious organizations, as they give way to new ones."[13]

As such, for these theorists, the situation of Christianity in Europe (and presumably the West) is not a terminal one. Rather, Britain is merely phasing from an out-dated, sluggish religious economy into a new, vibrant one that appeals to the British populace.[14] Soon, the weak, lifeless churches will be replaced with ones that offer greater appeal and usefulness than the former.

Not completely satisfied with either of these assertions, several scholars have promoted the notion of an even more inclusive and spiritually holistic approach to religion and spirituality. The school of scholars whose approach follows what can be termed the *Spiritual Revolution* thesis, represented by scholars like Heelas, Roof, and Woodhead, takes a more optimistic, broader attitude.[15]

To these theorists, the religious world is not diminishing in size; rather, the religious world is spilling over from traditional forms into new, personally-subjective avenues. Furthermore, one-sided, determinist theories concerning religious decline are being supplanted by theories offering a more multifaceted and multidimensional understanding of how and why religious beliefs are exercised. It is not that religion is dying; people are just as spiritual as before—in the modern age they are merely expressing their faiths in non-standard forms.

This theoretical position was the springboard for an investigation of religious life in Oregon because it seemed better to explain contemporary religious life in the Pacific Northwest. Many accepted sociological theories of religion do not adequately clarify the current (and historical) religious activity and expression of faith of Oregonians. If religious activity thrives with unencumbered religious options (so Rational Choice Theory), then Oregon (and

13. Ibid., 43.
14. Heelas et al., *The Spiritual Revolution*, 68–74.
15. Gill, *The "Empty" Church Revisited*, 204.

the whole Pacific Northwest) should have a robust church scene because it has never had an established state religion or denominational restrictions/limitations for its citizens. Yet, despite this, Oregon (as with Washington) is one of least churched states in the US. Furthermore, if this lowered church activity is indicative of the effects of secularization, then there should be a dramatic shift from religious belief to disbelief. Still, there is a substantial percentage of Oregonians who still indicate they are faithful Christians.[16]

The Spiritual Revolution theory appeared to work well in understanding current religious life in Oregon, but it, too, had problems. If people, at least generationally, were abandoning traditional Christian activities for religiously alternative ones, then one would expect to find the holistic milieu to be growing in Oregon; the data collected in the McMinnville Project sociological investigation suggests otherwise.[17]

Such sociological realities in Oregon make determining the depth and actuality of the religious scene difficult. New theories that focus on radical individualism in modern society (including Heelas, *et al.*) come closer to explaining the religious status in Oregon, but they also appear to fall short of a full understanding of the religious and spiritual citizens of that state (and others) in the United States of America. As Roof states of the Pacific Northwest, "The region has a distinctively secular ethos. It has a lasting legacy shaped by a frontier heritage with its individualism, free thinking, and religious indifference."[18]

In particular, Oregon provides an excellent case study of Christian growth, decline, and transformation; in many ways, it is unique; and in others, it is similar to other regions in western society. Demographically, Oregon is a medium-sized state with a smaller population than other areas of the United States.[19] It is

16. "Oregon," *Hometownusa.com*; online: http://www.hometownusa.com/or/.

17. See chapter 4 for more information on the presence of the holistic milieu in McMinnville society.

18. Roof, *Religion & Public Life in the Pacific Region*, 169.

19. According to the 2000 Census, Oregon's population is 3,521,515;

not a demographic hub like California or New York, but neither is it isolated from technology or culture. Indeed, it is these moderate circumstances that offered a unique opportunity to test both modern British and American theories of growth and decline. This investigation is needed and valuable.

Heelas *et al.* assert, "Whilst there are many excellent studies of Christianity on which we can draw in this task, there are, however, only a few that are directly focused on the issues which concern us the most."[20] In a way, Oregon can be seen as a control group, removed from many of the tainting forces of other frenzied social centers, which is relevant to the modern question of religious growth and decline.

1.2 The Sacro-States

"Diverse forms of religion exist in every society,"[21] Tamney reports. Historical records have detailed the variegated religious affiliation, participation, and power throughout the western world and into its spheres of influence.[22] Though there have been exceptions to societal acquiescence and obligation to religious involvement throughout the centuries, the general pattern historically has been one of overall adherence (voluntary or forced) to the church institution in the western world.[23] As Heelas *et al.* put it, Christians have enjoyed a " . . . life lived in terms of external or 'objective' roles, duties and obligations."[24] Organized religion, specifically Christianity, has been traditionally accepted by western society as

---

California's population is 35,116,033; Alaska's population is 648,818; online: http://quickfacts.census.gov/qfd/.

20. Heelas et al., *The Spiritual Revolution*, 7.

21. Tamney, *The Resilience of Conservative Religion*, 5.

22. See Gonzalez, *The Story of Christianity, Vol. 1 and Vol. 2*; Olson, *The Story of Christian Theology: Twenty Centuries of Tradition & Reform*; McGrath, *An Introduction to Christianity*, 235.

23. Gill, *The "Empty" Church Revisited*, 2–3; Aldridge, *Religion in the Contemporary World*, 2.

24. Heelas et al., *The Spiritual Revolution*, 2.

good and beneficial to society for centuries.[25] However, it was not always so, and it may not be so, presently.

With this in mind, four recurrent expressions of Christianity (what I term Sacro-Theism, Sacro-Communalism, Sacro-Clericalism, and Sacro-Egoism) are proposed and explained. These approaches to religion are defined relative to different forms of authority. How much or how intense each one manifests itself in society depends upon the time period and/or culture. It needs to be stated that these Sacro-States are more descriptive than prescriptive. Social science merely seeks to understand how religious institutions, customs, and movements operate—not to promote a particular social agenda (although for pastors that might be a viable option according to their religious mores). There are clues to the presence or dominance of one Sacro-State form or another, but it is likely that all of these approaches to religion are in effect in western society at the same time (although one might be more central in society over the others depending upon the historical period).

Sacro-Theism relates to where primary authority is given to direct revelation/calling(s) from God in people's lives, Sacro-Communalism focuses on non-denominational, non-institutional, unofficial religious beliefs (including the family or small groups), Sacro-Clericalism centers on ecclesiastical hierarchy and institutions, and Sacro-Egoism concentrates on the ultimate authority of the individual in spiritual matters. They all have their historical origins in Christianity, and they are all present in the modern religious world in varying intensity and manifestations.

1.2.1 Sacro-Theism

The origins of the Christian community began with the belief that God, through Jesus Christ, his Son and co-member of the Trinity,[26]

---

25. Barton, *The Practical Benefit of Christianity*.

26. Even though there are hints to the Trinity in the Old and New Testaments (Genesis 1:2, Matthew 3:16), the official Trinitarian doctrine was not established or endorsed until CE 362. See Gonzalez, *The Story of Christianity*,

directly revealed themselves to humanity (Sacro-Theism) in order
to provide a way to heal the problem of human sin and separation
from God (seen in Apostle Paul's New Testament epistles and later,
St. Augustine and his understanding of original sin).[27] Through Jesus, God imparted to his Disciples " . . . the way, and the truth, and
the life,"[28] and they listened and obeyed—God was their ultimate
authority and his words and commands displaced all else.

"Sacro-Theism," as with the other Sacro-States, is not just
a first-century-approach to Christianity; it is evident in other
historical periods of western civilization such as in the Mystical movement in thirteenth-century Germany.[29] Many Christian
movements focused on the words, beliefs, and practices of these
men and women—people such as Jesus, the Apostle Paul, Saint
Augustine, Teresa of Avila, Hildegard of Bingen, George Fox, etc.
who had a divine, direct communication from God. Accordingly,
anyone who gives primary authority to mystical encounters and
directly perceived revelation from God is a Sacro-Theist.

The description Tamney gives to one of the pastors in his
study of conservative religion is a good example of Sacro-Theism.
Tamney states, "He is led by the [Holy] Spirit and he challenges
people. The pastor says what he wants because God works through
him. He might abruptly stop a sermon and do something different
because he feels that is what God wanted him to do."[30]

In defining what beliefs and practices a Sacro-Theistic approach would exclude, Sacro-Theists tend to downplay the authority of human authority in their lives as being open to corruption;
just because a pastor says it is so does not make it so. Beliefs must
have their origin and affirmation directly in God. Also, Sacro-
Theists take a humble, self-deprecating view of their own spiritual
authority, because as humans, they, too, are open to temptation

27. Apostle Paul, *Romans 5:12-22*; St. Augustine of Hippo, *De nupt. et con-
cup., II, xxvi, 43.*

28. John 14:6, *The Holy Bible* (NASB).

29. Gonzalez, *The Story of Christianity*, Vol 1, 356–359.

30. Tamney, *The Resilience of Conservative Religion*, 89.

and bad judgment. Their motto is two-fold: "Trust in the LORD with all your heart And do not lean on your own understanding"[31] and "do not store your treasures on earth, where moths and rust destroy and where thieves break in and steal."[32]

As a simple example, a Sacro-Theist might opt for opening the Bible at whatever page it fell to and reading to find out God's special message for him/her. What matters most is God's direct, revealed truth in their minds, to the dismissal of all else, no matter how rational or reasonable or fashionable.

1.2.2 Sacro-Communalism

"Sacro-Communalism" focuses on non-denominational and non-institutional group beliefs. Thus, Sacro-Communalism manifests itself by the belief system(s) of the lay community operating without instruction from an institution or religious hierarchy, and it exists outside of traditional, formal, and hierarchical control. The lay community directs religious life—not official church or denominational leaders. Institutional Christianity is contrary to the authentic Christian community of believers, which promotes egalitarianism alongside of theological truths.

Of course, any modern-day spirituality or religion that exists outside of institutional control or influence and utilizes a local community in its particular worship of God/the Divine could also be considered to be Sacro-Communal. The current "Hipster Movement" could easily be characterized as Sacro-Communal. Yet, Sacro-Communalism can quickly transform into Sacro-Clericalism when enough followers officially organize and expand their movement. Some church historians claim this happened with Christianity after the first century with officials dictating doctrine and liturgy not necessarily mandated or embraced in the first lay Christian communities.[33] Others think it occurred in Western

31. *The Holy Bible* (NASB), Proverbs 3:5.

32. *The Holy Bible* (NASB), Matthew 6:19.

33. Borg, "The Historian, the Christian, and Jesus," 10-11; Crossan, "A Tale of Two Gods," 1272.

Society during and after the Civil Rights Movement of the 1960s and 1970s.[34]

In defining what beliefs and practices they would exclude, Sacro-Communalists shy away from official organized events and regular meetings as being too political and contrived. They might prefer to meet in a coffee shop rather than a sanctuary. Additionally, formal creeds such as the Apostles' Creed, the Nicene Creed, and the Athanasian Creed would be considered more prescribed than God would want. One is not a Christian because one has gone through the Catechism or a five-week membership class.

To them, Scriptural evidence points to an informal way of religious life that is far removed from the hyperactive, rigid halls of institutional church. They would point out that Jesus normally ministered to people in their homes or in the countryside; and that even when he was in the Temple, it was normally to chastise the religious folk there for missing the point of religiosity and spirituality.

As a simple example, a Sacro-Communalist might opt for getting together with friends at dinner to discuss potential books (the Bible and extra-biblical sources, too) to read together in order to build up the group. As McCracken points out,

> Enter the age of the Christian hipster. As the '90s gave way to the 2000s, young evangelicals reared in the ostentatious Je$us subculture began to rebel. They sought a more intellectual faith, one that didn't reject outright the culture, ideas, and art of the secular world. In typical hipster fashion, they rejected the corporate mentality of the purpose-driven megachurch and McMansion evangelicalism, and longed for a simpler, back-to-basics faith that was more about serving the poor than serving Starbucks in the church vestibule.[35]

Sacro-Communalists push for an informal, non-official approach to religion wherein religious authority rests not in hierarchy

34. McCracken, "Hipster Faith;" online: http://www.christianitytoday.com /ct/2010/september/9.24.html?start=2.

35. Ibid.

but in an affirming and supportive community. With this in mind, one would expect to find responses in the survey data that pushed back against both religious milieus being too institutional or too individualistic. Sacro-Communalists responses would affirm an egalitarian approach to religiosity, with the community of believers loosely held together in altruistic brotherhood (or sisterhood).

1.2.3 Sacro-Clericalism

"Sacro-Clericalism" is defined by the development of an official church hierarchy, the acceptance of common creeds and doctrinal positions, the definition and development of denominational movements, even the construction of church buildings and offices—all detailing what it means to be a Christian, at least legitimately and corporately. Sacro-Clericalism can be seen in the form of legalistic, orchestrated worship and affiliation. Thus, for adherents, Sacro-Clericalism manifests itself in regular attendance, obedience to denominational codes, and fidelity to specific religious movements. It is more about the corporate understanding and expression of Christianity than an individual one. In fact, individualism is often shunned for its dangerous potential of division and heresy.

According to Gonzalez, during the Golden Age of Medieval Christianity, "Christendom most nearly approached the ideal of being 'one flock, under one shepherd.'"[36] McGrath claims, "By the fifth century, Christianity had begun to establish itself securely in the Mediterranean region. Five major centers emerged within the region, each of which served as the nucleus of groups of churches: Alexandria, Antioch, Constantinople, Jerusalem, and Rome."[37] Holding the title of a Christian required being under the authority of the church. This is the essence of Sacro-Clericalism—spiritual acquiescence to an ecclesiastical body.

As Tamney states,

---

36. Gonzalez, *The Story of Christianity*, Vol 1., 310.
37. McGrath, *An Introduction to Christianity*, 261.

> Traditionalists unquestionably affirm the authenticity of the Bible, seek to use the Bible as the only important foundation for their life, and proclaim the superiority of their own religion. The rightness of a person's morality is not determined by the sincerity of the individual's search for goodness but whether it conforms to the Bible.[38]

In defining what beliefs and practices a Sacro-Clericalist approach would exclude, Sacro-Clericalists find any approach to religion that circumvents institutional authority to be dangerous. Tamney states, "What traditionalists seek to preserve, above all, is valuing the group more than the individual, even to the point of being willing to kill someone who symbolizes a threat to the group or to that for which the group stands."[39]

Personal application of Scriptures is permitted, but Biblical interpretation must adhere to institutional, corporate understandings. New trends in religious worship or presentation are only acceptable if sanctioned and developed by the central church authorities. Additionally, church community mores are not just for Sunday, but are to be carried out at all times, regardless of whom one is with or where. The individual does not dictate what is appropriate religious belief and practice—Jesus gave the church that duty, specifically.

As a simple example, a Sacro-Clericalist might opt for a reading from the Bible that has been prescribed by the church leaders or denomination—lectionaries are good examples of this. Furthermore, specific Bible translations are only to be used; a smorgasbord of translations can only lead to misunderstanding and confusion.

Ironically, some modern-day churches may be attempting to implement a hybrid individualized yet corporate religious environment in lieu of a strictly traditionalist approach. Concerning one of the churches in his study of conservative religion, Tamney states, "The traditional service was perceived as a structure, a thing, to which church attendees were obligated to conform. At Spirited Church, the ritual fits the desires of the congregation. An

---

38. Tamney, *The Resilience of Conservative Religion*, 245.

39. Ibid., 8.

important aspect of the balanced ritual is that individuals have options."[40]

The bigger question is whether such an implementation is a new implementation or just another type of institutionalized religious ritual. Tamney goes on to say, "Spirited [Church] is run by the pastor, who, however, has created small groups within which the laity have considerable autonomy."[41] Thus, people in this church do have some power, but this autonomy is still regulated by the head of the church (the pastor) and is, therefore, still an institutional aspect.

For the Sacro-Clericalist, it is all about building up the community that exists within the traditional structure of church life. Thus, in the McMinnville Project data, there would be evidence of this presence, although perhaps not as strong as Sacro-Egoism or Sacro-Communalism based on recently noted trends of individualism and anti-institutionalism. As such, one would expect to see responses that affirmed denominational or church control, responses suggesting that too much emphasis is placed on the individual's right to believe whatever they want to believe, and responses elevating greater church matters (such as evangelism, missions, fund-raising, etc.) over personal matters. The organization is all; the individual is secondary.

1.2.4 Sacro-Egoism

As theological thought changed, specifically after the advent of liberalism in the nineteenth century,[42] a change began to take place in the religious world. Religious attitudes and prioritization seem to begin shifting from Sacro-Clericalism, where authority is given to the church and its representatives, to Sacro-Egoism, where the individual assumes greatest authority. The role of the individual, the self, was elevated more than ever before and self-reliance was

---

40. Ibid., 87.

41. Ibid., 109.

42. Richardson, *History Sacred and Profane*, 121–124.

glamorized, epitomized, and utilized in society—even until the present. Liberal theologians like Schleiermacher, Ritschl, and Tillich " . . . sought to anchor that faith in common human experience, and interpret it in ways that made sense within the modern worldview."[43] Schleiermacher, known as the "Father of Modern Liberal Theology,"[44] considered religion and Christianity to be " . . . the distinctly human awareness of something infinite beyond the self on whom the self is dependent for everything."[45]

Though first a subtle and infrequent occurrence, more and more the authority and centrality of the church began to lose ground to the prominence of the individual. Culturally, the expression of religion and Christianity encountered " . . . a turn towards life lived by reference to one's own subjective experiences (relational as much as individualistic)."[46] Leaning on one's own understanding became an asset, not a detriment, to religious life and approval. According to Heelas and Woodhead, "The subjectivities of each individual become a, if not the, unique source of significance, meaning and authority."[47] Grasso continues this understanding stating, "Liberalism's movement toward an ever deeper individualism receives signal expression in the ascendancy of the type of liberalism that dominates our intellectual scene, in the ascendancy . . . termed the liberalism of the unencumbered self."[48]

Starks and Robinson comment that modernists " . . . see individuals and not a deity as the ultimate arbiters of moral authority and hold to a largely individually directed universe."[49] Religious focus moved from the institution to the individual leading up to the civil rights movement(s) of the 1960s.

43. McGrath, *Historical Theology*, 233.

44. Gerrish, *Prince of the Church*, xi.

45. Olson, *The Story of Christian Theology*, 544.

46. Heelas et al., *The Spiritual Revolution*, 2.

47. Ibid., 3–4.

48. Grasso, "Christianity, Enlightenment Liberalism, and the Quest for Freedom," 304.

49. Starks and Robinson, "Moral Cosmology, Religion, and Adult Values for Children," 32.

Sacro-Egoism refers to the situation in which the self or ego has the highest sacred authority in a person's life, giving direction and meaning to religious and spiritual activities (or non-participation). God and religion are seen more as "helpers" to individual spiritual fulfillment in life. Tamney remarks that modern society, " . . . while it accepts a modern civic code, a fragmented culture, and church-state separation, also puts the individual at the center of spirituality (each of us should form a personal religion, combining fragments from various traditions)."[50] Personal commitment is key in Sacro-Egoism; people utilizing this approach take their religious and spiritual lives very seriously and purposefully. Sacro-Egoism is not just found in traditional church settings; it is also evident in the holistic milieu and unchurched milieu in McMinnville, Oregon.

In defining what beliefs and practices they would exclude, Sacro-Egoists consider the church to be a good starting place for biblical interpretation and application, but not the ultimate source—that source rests within themselves. Sacro-Egoists would also shy away from liturgical events that restrict their expressions of faith. Such events would only limit their God-given freedom of religion. As a common example, Sacro-Egoists might opt for a reading from the Bible that reached them personally and helped them in situations relevant to their personal life circumstances. Sacro-Egoism pushes the individual's needs and control in front of all other variables in religious life.

With the previously mentioned in mind, substantiation would be apparent in the McMinnville Project survey responses to indicate a Sacro-Egoistical approach to religion. One would expect Sacro-Egoists to claim themselves as the highest spiritual authority in their lives and would downplay church institutional power over the individual. They would indicate a high prioritization of their faith and would have shopped around for churches that best fit their own needs. They would be involved in religious/spiritual activities outside of the church that develop their personal spirituality. They would not limit themselves to traditional avenues of religious activity and be open to trying new alternative forms of

50. Tamney, *The Resilience of Conservative Religion*, 39.

religious expression. A cluster of survey responses such as these, focusing on empowering the individual and the cultivation of their spiritual life, would be a clear indication of Sacro-Egoism.

1.3 Sacro-Egoism and Individualization, Subjectivization, and Privatization

Amongst the prominent theories as to the explanation of this apparent change in religious life, several camps of thought have emerged—the Secularization theorists, the Rational Choice theorists, and those associated with the Spiritual Revolution thesis. Not surprisingly, considering the complexity of religion in society, these groups are not in agreement with each other; however, they do share a common notion in that they all suggest that the religious change that has taken place inextricably involves the growing prominence of the individual in western society. This factor is evident in the current subjectivization, autonomization, and privatization studies of religion; and there is much in these current trends to tie-in with Sacro-Egoism.

The role of the individual, with the subjectivities and newfound power of choice, has direct connections and agreement with much in the Sacro-Egoism understanding of religiosity. There are also key differences as well in how preeminent scholars—Taylor, Heelas, Woodhead, Bellah, Hammond, and Wilson—understand the role and significance of the individual and church life in modernity. These are considered in turn.

1.3.1 Charles Taylor

Regarding Charles Taylor, Sacro-Egoism matches up well with his understanding of modern religiosity when he states, "To take my religion seriously is to take it personally, more devotionally, inwardly, more committedly."[51] Personal choice is a key ingredient in Sacro-Egoism.

51. Taylor, *Varieties of Religion Today*, 11.

Personal relevance is another factor in Sacro-Egoism; religious and spiritual activity must have meaning for it to be embraced. These notions are substantiated by the data collected in the McMinnville Project; however, Taylor also remarks,

> There are people who have an original, powerful experience, which then gets communicated through some kind of institution; it gets handed on to others, and they tend to live it in a kind of secondhand way. In the transmission, the force and intensity of the original tends to get lost, until all that remains is "dull habit."[52]

This notion contends with Sacro-Egoism, which, as mentioned above, suggests that people who still attend church do care about what they believe, and that religious actions have intense personal meaning and significance to them.

Another ingredient of Sacro-Egoism involves freedom for all individuals to find their own spiritual path, but this does not necessarily mean that they will not or cannot be in community with each other. In fact, tolerance for individual beliefs is a crucial element in Sacro-Egoism; if anything, Sacro-Egoism will be more enabling of collective connections despite disagreements. This, too, is substantiated by the data collected in the McMinnville Project.

1.3.2 Paul Heelas and Linda Woodhead

Heelas et al.'s description of the Spiritual Revolution and Sacro-Egoism are also not necessarily at odds with each other as sociological models. Heelas et al. also state, "Some of the longitudinal data we have cited would appear to indicate that inner-life beliefs have overtaken, or are overtaking, beliefs more obviously belonging to a traditional theistic frame of reference."[53] This is substantiated again in the McMinnville Project data findings. Individuals care deeply about their spiritual lives even if their involvement in traditional or alternative spirituality is low.

52. Ibid., 5.
53. Heelas et al., *The Spiritual Revolution*, 74.

Furthermore, the assertion of Heelas that

> Spirituality is experienced as dwelling within the here-and-now; as integral to life; as inseparable from, a natural aspect of, what it is to be alive. Rather than merely relying on external sources of significance or authority, considerable importance is attached to the voice of experience; experience which emanates from the heart of one's subjective-life, ultimately from ones's life-itself,[54]

has reverberations with Sacro-Egoism, which also affirms that people take particular, non-orchestrated (but tangible) steps to exercise their personalized religious understanding.

Additionally, Sacro-Egoism suggests that people care about their spiritual lives and relationships with the Divine. There is a subjective turn to the individual, as Heelas *et al.* suggest, but how much of this turn is to the holistic milieu is debatable. The holistic milieu is just one aspect of the expression of Sacro-Egoism and Sacro-Communalism by people in the McMinnville Project.

Rather than previous institutional or Sacro-Clerical admonishment or condemnation of non-traditional activities, modern western society is more tolerant for personal expression and experimentation specifically encountered in the holistic milieu. Yet, the low numbers of holistic milieu participants and their subsequent inaccessibility in the West limit sociological investigation.

Thus, the assertion of Heelas *et al* that "cultural renderings of holistic themes . . . will increasingly take over the role once played by having been brought up in the Christian faith"[55] is not necessarily in agreement with Sacro-Egoism. Their prediction is a definite possibility; however, the Sacro-Egoism understanding of the holistic milieu is that it falls into the category of freedom of individual examination, which may or may not end as acceptance. Sacro-egoists can equally well be at home within permissive churches or as shoppers in the religious marketplace.

---

54. Heelas, "The Infirmity Debate: On the Viability of New Age Spiritualities of Life," 224.

55. Heelas et al., *The Spiritual Revolution*, chapter 5.

1.3.3 Robert Bellah

Sacro-Egoism complements Bellah's description of the modern approach to religious institutionalism. He states, "Commoner among religious individualist than criticism of religious beliefs is criticism of institutional religion, or the church as such. Hypocrisy is one of the most frequent charges against organized religion."[56]

Bellah continues,

> Far more serious than any of the startling events of the decade was the massive erosion of the legitimacy of American institutions—business, government, education, the churches, the family—that set in, particularly among young people, and that continues, if public opinion polls are to be believed, in the 1970s even when overt protest has become less frequent.[57]

Sacro-Egoism pushes back against the corporate approach to faith, which has been, at times, contrived, forced, and neglectful of the individual lives of its parishioners.

Bellah's notion that people seek to maintain personal balance in their religious lives lines up with Sacro-Egoism. He states,

> Recognizing that we are all, of whatever race and gender, tempted to exalt our own imperial egos above all else, we can still find those social contexts and those traditions of interpretation, which can moderate that egoism and offer a different understanding of personal fulfillment.[58]

One aspect that Bellah is not in agreement with Sacro-Egoism concerns his appraisal of the modern individualistic society. Bellah remarks,

> Just when we are moving to an ever-greater validation of the sacredness of the individual person, our capacity to imagine a social fabric that would hold individuals

56. Bellah et al., *Habits of the Heart*, 234.

57. Bellah, "New Religious Consciousness: Rejecting the Past, Designing the Future," 33–41.

58. Bellah, "Is There a Common American Culture?," 613.

together is vanishing. This is in part because of the fact
that the religious individualism that I have been describing is linked to an economic individualism, which, ironically, knows nothing of the sacredness of the individual.[59]

This is contrary to Sacro-Egoism's claim of self-awareness
and nurturing that goes on in modern religious and spiritual life.
Sacro-Egoism asserts that people take measure to investigate,
understand, and cultivate their religious lives. Moreover, Bellah's
claim that " . . . the mindless rationalization of means and the lack
of concern with ends would only increase as biblical religion and
morality continue to erode,"[60] seems extremely pessimistic and is
not supported by the research data. Sacro-Egoism suggests that
people care about their religious lives and seek ways to improve
upon its depth and significance—this is mindful, purposeful, and
edifying to them.

Additionally, Bellah remarks, "Individual conviction and
conscience have become the standards relative to which even
long-established practices can be overturned."[61] This is not evident
in Sacro-Egoism; in fact, the McMinnville Project data suggests
that some "long-established practices," such as reading the Bible
and praying, are still just as valued and honored by individuals in
modern society. People still care a great deal about their spiritual
and religious lives, evidentially.

1.3.4 Phillip Hammond

Hammond's approach to religion also often connects and disagrees
with Sacro-Egoism. Regarding church participation, Hammond
claims,

> If, in such areas—the far West is, perhaps, the notable
> example—the church is less an expression of community

59. Ibid., 613.

60. Bellah, "New Religious Consciousness: Rejecting the Past, Designing
the Future."

61 Bellah, "Is There a Common American Culture?," 213.

than an individual's choice of activity, then the dispro-
portionate number who are evangelical and non-denominational is better understood. Being "Christian" for such
people is not the result of inherited community ties but
an aggressively achieved, individual status.[62]

Sacro-Egoism would affirm that church participation is more
about individual choice in the present society than in previous
decades or centuries. People go to church (or not) because they
feel less social pressure to conform to a religious ideal outside of
themselves.

Hammond's approach to religion diverges from Sacro-Egoism in his understanding of the relationship between autonomy
and involvement. Hammond states,

> The question can therefore be asked if, as we would
> expect, those high in personal autonomy are found dis-
> proportionately among those reporting reduced involve-
> ment, while those low in personal autonomy are found
> disproportionately among those reporting increased
> involvement . . . The answer is a resounding Yes to the
> question.[63]

Sacro-Egoism does not make the assertion that autonomy
leads to reduced church involvement although it is a possibility. In
Sacro-Egoism, religious and spiritual autonomy leads to a deepening, not thinning of religious belief for many people. As mentioned
earlier regarding Taylor, tolerance of new beliefs and expressions
of religion is embraced for oneself and for others in Sacro-Egoism.

1.3.5 Bryan Wilson

Sacro-Egoism pushes against Wilson's approach to secularization and privatization but is not completely at odds with it. He
states, "Religion becomes a matter of choice, but whatever religion

---

62. Hammond, "Religion and the Persistence of Identity," 9.

63. Hammond, *Religion and Personal Autonomy*, 77.

is chosen is of no consequence to the operation of the social system."[64] Sacro-Egoism would affirm this notion and say that the response is movement toward individualistic religious authority over the institution.

Individual choice is a hallmark of Sacro-Egoism, and the shifting sociological reality is that general society no longer revolves around religion or Christianity. Furthermore, there is no conflict between Sacro-Egoism and Wilson's assessment of church life. "That the course of modern society proceeds influenced in only the slightest of ways by such differences in expressed religious behaviour illustrates how marginal religious institutions have, in fact become."[65]

Yet, Wilson and Sacro-Egoism are in tension when he states, "Men act less and less in response to religious motivation."[66] Sacro-Egoism challenges this assertion suggesting that lowered church membership does not necessarily equate with unresponsiveness to religious motivation. Perhaps people are now responding to new forms of religious expression that meets more of their individual needs than their community needs. Perhaps they are allowed more than ever to be directors of their own spiritual pilgrimage—one that brings them to a closer relationship with God or a higher sense of spiritual fulfillment in their lives.

Additionally, Wilson claims, "Sociology appropriately regards religion as primarily an institutional phenomenon."[67] Such a restricted view of religion in human lives can only lead to a negative conclusion considering institutional membership numbers. The idea of Sacro-Egoism suggests that religious life is currently more about individualism than corporate worship and faith.

Finally, Wilson states, "Individuals cannot confer sacredness; the sense that things are sacred is a socially communicated apprehension, the origins of which perhaps defy analysis."[68] Sacro-

64. Wilson, "The Return of the Sacred," 277.
65. Wilson, *Religion in Secular Society*, 12.
66. Ibid., 10.
67. Wilson, *Religion in Secular Society*, 18.
68. Wilson, "The Return of the Sacred," 278.

Egoism and subjectivization theorists would challenge this, based on studies suggesting the contrary. People can, and do, bestow sacredness on things atypical and untraditional, both in the congregational and holistic milieus.

It would be incorrect to say that Sacro-Egoism supplants individualization, subjectivization, and privatization for these religious realities are an important part of Sacro-Egoism and help shape its expression and existence. However, Sacro-Egoism is more than just any one of these notions—it incorporates individualization and subjectivization in part, and rejects or embraces privatization (depending on the individual's attitude), reflecting the complexity of religious/spiritual experience for the individual in modern western culture.

It shares the focus and prioritization of the individual with individualization, which leads to personalized, directed behaviors, beliefs, and attitudes about religion and spirituality. It includes the personally-relevant "Subjective-Turn" that allows people to concentrate on and enhance their inner religious lives outside of the corporate experience. It affirms the modern privatization of religion that has taken religious power away from the institutions and placed it into the hands of the individuals in society.

Each of the aforementioned theorists and their assertions confirm and are in tension with certain aspects of Sacro-Egoism. However, as the axiom goes, "The proof is in the pudding," and thus, the McMinnville Project adds credence and validation to the concepts upon which Sacro-Egoism rests. Clearly, the data supports the notion of Sacro-Egoism. The results of this sociological study of religiosity in Oregon are examined in the following chapters.

1.4 Conclusion

Religious life in the modern world is markedly different than fifty years ago. According to Tamney, "Modernization theory assumes that we are part of a historical process dating back to premodern times."[69] Currently, this process is changing as can be observed in a variety of ways as mentioned earlier, most visibly in lowered membership and attendance numbers. This situation has been attributed to poor religious offerings, to a modern emphasis on the secular world, to ineffective participation and devotion of believers worldwide, or to the will of God (in some religious circles).[70] While all these may be partially true, the danger is making a synecdoche of the products of decline and over-estimating their importance and influence in religion.

Not surprisingly, many scholars have begun to question the wisdom and absoluteness of recent theories of decline. Robin Gill writes, "To focus so exclusively upon declining Christian participation and beliefs may be to miss other religious forms brought with new immigrants or re-emerging within the indigenous population."[71] Anastasia Karaflogka states, "A new theoretical and methodological field is needed which will address religious, cultural, social and anthropological issues as they arise."[72] Heelas *et al.* offer, "The declining influence of religion—particularly Christianity—in western societies has been the chief topic of the study of religion for over a century, but in recent years the emergence of something called 'spirituality' has—increasingly—demanded attention."[73] Martyn Percy states, "Religion, especially with Christianity in mind, possesses the capacity to be resilient within modernity, both resisting and accommodating contemporary culture in dynamic inter-relationality."[74] Christian Smith proclaims, "I do not believe Christianity will become extinct any time soon."[75]

69. Tamney, *The Resilience of Conservative Religion*, 245.

70. Hatcher, "Saved by Grace V—Election, Free Will, Fairness, and Evangelism;" online: http://www.eefweb.org/sermons/topical/Saved%20By%20Grace/Election%20Free%20Will%20Fairness%20and%20Evangelism.htm.

71. Gill, *The "Empty" Church Revisited*, 212.

72. Karaflogka, "Religion on—Religion in Cyberspace," 200.

73. Heelas et al., *The Spiritual Revolution*, 9–10.

74. Percy, *The Salt of the Earth*, 346.

75. Smith, "Why Christianity Works: An Emotions-Focused Phenomenological Account," 177.

These scholars present the reality of current religious growth and decline both in the world, in Oregon, and in the Pacific Northwest.

What is needed is an accurate evaluation of the state of religion and the attitudes of its remaining adherents—one that looks deeper than the surface, one that sees beyond numerical statistics, and one that perceives individuals in their distinctiveness. The McMinnville Project sought to discover if there was a transformation of religiosity occurring in modernity in the west. The notion it investigated was whether or not the majority of people there were still deeply committed to their religious and spiritual lives (and personally active, somehow) despite lowered church membership and participation figures—the Sacro-Egoism assertion—and whether they were embracing the holistic milieu over traditional religious avenues. The testing of the hypothesis began with the selection of McMinnville, Oregon as the sample group, and was followed by the administration of demographic analysis, statistical surveys, and interviews based on its comparison group study—the Kendal Project.

With this in mind, chapter two provides a brief overview of Heelas and Woodhead's choice of towns to research and their methodology and goals for the Kendal case study. Likewise, chapter two explains the choice of McMinnville, Oregon, as a case study and the methodology and goals used in uncovering the state of Christian and religious thought in that unassuming city.

_____ 2 _____

The McMinnville Project

2.0 Introduction

IN THE PREVIOUS CHAPTER, different sociological theories of religion concerning the state of spiritual faith and Christianity in the West were introduced and explained. The conclusions and speculations of three schools of thought were examined—the Secularists, the Rational Choice theorists, and theorists associated with the Spiritual Revolutionists.

One study, in particular, stood out significantly regarding religious life in the United States as a compelling approach to the question of growth and decline in religion/spirituality, that of Paul Heelas *et al.* In their study, they state, "With growth continuing, but possibly slowing down somewhat, our prediction is that weekly participation in the milieu will double in size over the next 40 or 50 years to take in a little more than 3 percent of the population of the nation."[1] However, they continue, "The developments highlighted here [in *The Spiritual Revolution*] mean that growth may continue at a high rate—high enough to bring about a spiritual revolution."[2] Heelas *et al.* also remark that it would help to understand religious life in general if a similar study was undertaken in America as well.

1. Heelas et al., *The Spiritual Revolution*, 137.
2. Ibid., 138.

In their orchestration of the Kendal project, Heelas and Woodhead established a "Sequence of Tasks."[3] These included 1) choosing an appropriate research site; 2) mapping the city's religious associations, visiting each and every congregation, and determining the denominational histories; 3) identifying and defining who would be researched as representative case studies; 4) a systematic counting of all religious membership in traditional places of worship; 5) the distribution of questionnaires to the traditional churches; 6) mapping of the city's holistic milieu; 7) the distribution of questionnaires to the holistic milieu centers; 8) in-depth interviews with subjects from both the congregational and holistic milieu studies; 9) and participating in a street survey to investigate the people who do not go to either church or alternative spiritual centers.

Similarly, the McMinnville Project followed the same classification of tasks to investigate the state of religion in this "heartland" city in Oregon. These elements of the McMinnville Project research design are considered in turn. Somewhat ironically, this chapter provides the details of my own individual investigation of religiosity in the West, providing more personal anecdotes to what transpired during my research project and what to make of it, sociologically.

2.1 The Choice of Kendal and McMinnville as a Case Study

Heelas *et al.* chose the northern English town of Kendal to research their theory mainly because of its "practicality."[4] It was geographically close to the researchers and was a "self-contained town,"[5] its population was modest enough to handle both in terms of management and diversity, and it was well-defined religiously in

---

3. Ibid., 152.

4. Heelas et al., *The Spiritual Revolution*, 151.

5. Ibid., 151.

regards to traditional and non-traditional expressions of faith. As such, it fitted their needs well as a research site.

Likewise, the town of McMinnville was chosen as a case study in Oregon. Several other cities were considered—Albany, Corvallis, Eugene, Hillsboro, Medford, Newberg, Portland, Salem—but McMinnville was a far better match to Kendal than most possible locations.

McMinnville, like Kendal, was chosen for its "practicality"[6] in that it was less than twenty minutes away from this researcher's home and most of the team of volunteers. This enabled frequent trips "into the field" and to facilitate "Super Sunday."[7] Furthermore, it was similar in population size to Kendal—in 2005, Mc-Minnville had 29,200 citizens[8] and Kendal had a population of 28,000 citizens;[9] and, like Kendal, McMinnville is a "relatively self-contained market town."[10]

Demographically, McMinnville shares Kendal's characteristic of a homogeneous community. Over 80 percent of its citizens are white/Caucasian with the next biggest demographic group being the Hispanic community that makes up near 15 percent of the population.[11]

2.2 Mapping the Churches

Once McMinnville had been selected as the case city, a thorough examination of its churches and spiritual meeting places began. The first goal was to find out the number and names of these different religious buildings of worship and/or religious centers. The second goal was to determine what sort of religious offerings were available for McMinnvillians. The third goal was to find the

6. Ibid.

7. This is the term that was used when referring to the demographic, latitudinal study on April 23, 2006 by Knox and the volunteers.

8. Online: http://www.mcminnville.org/aboutMcminnville.asp.

9. Heelas et al., *The Spiritual Revolution*, 49.

10. Ibid., 8.

11. Online: http://www.city-data.com/city/McMinnville-Oregon.html.

locations, addresses, and meeting times of all the churches and congregations. The fourth goal was to begin the screening/selection process for the case study churches and religious centers that would receive the surveys on "Super Sunday."

Finding an initial list of churches in McMinnville was relatively easy—a quick Google search[12] offered several different Internet sites that provided a lengthy directory of places of worship in McMinnville and its just-out-of-city-limits settlements. Several churches listed had either disbanded or moved to a new location within the city (such as the Friends Church of McMinnville, which dissolved a few years earlier).[13] Thus, an initial list of thirty-nine churches was reduced to twenty-eight places of worship.

2.2.1 Case Study Churches

Once the list had been created of churches in McMinnville, a search began to determine which churches fitted into the case study categories. A preliminary Internet search of each church's website was undertaken (where they had a website) to read over their *Statement of Belief's* page. This provided a crucial clue to their varying religious dispositions; yet, it was only the beginning step in finding out what they believed and with what type of congregation they were aligned.

Several letters of inquiry and permission were sent to potential churches that matched up with the available congregation types. The McMinnville Project and my involvement were explained in brief, and the pastors were asked if they would like to hear more about the project goals and expectations, and on whether or not they might wish to participate in the study.

If willing, and once contact was made, in order to ensure a proper "fit" for each case, a short summary was read or spoken to the pastor(s) of each different congregational type,[14] and they

12. Online: http://www.Google.com.

13. Dick, Northwest Yearly Meeting Area Superintendent, email message to author (July 18, 2006).

14. Heelas et al., *The Spiritual Revolution*, 17–19.

were asked if that sounded like their congregation. The congregational types, as identified by Woodhead and Heelas, were "Congregations of Difference"—predominantly Evangelical in their practices; "Congregations of Experiential Difference"—predominantly Charismatic/Evangelical; "Congregations of Humanity"—predominantly mainline liberal denominations; "Congregations of Experiential Humanity"—predominantly non-liturgical, Unitarian, or Quaker; and the "Holy Roman Catholic Church"—the largest denominational group in America with over 50,000,000 in membership.[15]

2.3 Churches: The Count

As with the Kendal Project, the McMinnville Project began its study with a massive demographic count of church attendance on a specific Sunday. Nearly sixty volunteers stood in close proximity to the entrances of twenty-eight different churches to see who was attending them. The goal was to count as effectively and accurately as possible who was attending church on that particular Sunday.

2.3.1 Informed Consent

Because showing up unannounced with clipboards, positioning ourselves near every entrance, and taking count of each individual walking in might have most likely offended the churches' sense of privacy and possibly incurred the wrath of the police, advanced notice of the project was sent out to every place of worship.

Several churches responded immediately, both in positive and negative form. Five church pastors called me to give their enthusiastic permission to do the demographic count on Super Sunday. Furthermore, the denominational range of the assenters was across the board, from liturgical to confessional to Pentecostal. Several churches emailed me to let me know they would be more than willing to participate; however, not every communication

15. Online: http://www.adherents.com/rel_.html#Pew_branches.

was in the affirmative. A few responses were quite harsh and pro-hibitive. For these churches, I assured them all either on the phone or by email that under no circumstances would any volunteer tied to the project step foot on their church property.

Any counting that would take place at the non-participating churches would be unobtrusively "off-property" on public prop-erty. Volunteers could sit in their cars on the street and count the people walking in during the service(s) without interference or interruption. In other words, even while these churches did not want to take part in the survey, the research was able to include a general count of these congregations. Thus, the non-participating churches maintained their expressed desire for privacy, and no promises or laws were broken.

All-in-all, about 75 percent of the churches on the list con-sented to having volunteers present on Super Sunday to take the count, and of the remaining 25 percent of churches, only half of those said, "No." The others did not respond to either the letters, emails, or my voice-mail messages. It was assumed that they were not averse to participation, and volunteers were sent to these churches, aware they might be showing up to a hostile crowd, even though none were rebuked for their presence on Sunday.

2.3.2 Super Sunday

The long months of groundwork and planning were evident when Super Sunday arrived for the McMinnville Project. This prepara-tion was a necessary element for this comparative study of the religion/spirituality of McMinnville because, unlike the Kendal Project, which had a team of five members to "divide and conquer" the business of the Count and the surveys, I was alone in the man-agement and implementation of the study with the assistance of some personally-trained volunteers. However, the whole day went by without even one problem with the helpers, the participating and non-participating churches, transportation, or the collection of the count sheets.

The McMinnville Project volunteers visited twenty-eight churches on Super Sunday and counted 5,789 people in attendance that day, both in the morning and evening services. Additionally, so that no congregation was left out of the Count, the Seventh-Day Adventist Church was counted on the following Saturday. The final tally, therefore, showed twenty-nine churches visited that week for a total of 5,963 people attending church in McMinnville.

2.4 Churches: Survey Questionnaires

These questionnaires were utilized to provide a broad understanding of the state of Christianity within McMinnville city limits. The hope was to gather information from a wide variety of religious environments, not just traditional avenues where religion would automatically be considered a high priority. Another benefit of these surveys was that they provided the avenue of possibility for interviewing willing candidates. A section was provided on the back of each survey for the participants to fill out with contact information if they would not mind being contacted about the survey and their religious beliefs.

2.4.1 Survey Design and Translation

In order to accommodate Heelas and Woodhead's request (hope) for "reliable evidence,"[16] the surveys were kept as similar as possible. It was assumed that "respondents from different backgrounds will understand questions in the same way and be able to respond 'from the same place'"[17] with minimal adjustment to the language of the survey. Thus, there were some specific modifications in the surveys questions.

The list of Kendal churches was substituted with the churches present in McMinnville. Examples of American church-affiliated

16. Heelas et al., *The Spiritual Revolution*, 60.

17. Homan and Dandelion, "The Religious Basis of Resistance and Non-Response: A Methodological Note," 205.

and independent groups were provided instead of British ones. Issues of terminology, political affiliation, and cultural idioms were adjusted; however, substitutions were made with the notion of keeping as close as possible to Heelas and Woodhead's understandings.

Several civic groups mentioned in the Kendal project do not exist in the United States although America does have groups with similar goals/characteristics. Yet, providing parallel political bodies was not as important as providing a relevant list that Oregonians would know and understand.

The remainder of the questions was left alone, without alteration. It was assumed that people would understand the general meaning of questions regarding spiritual/religious practices, ultimate authority, importance of faith, etc. A few of the references could be considered obscure,[18] but that was an additional aspect of investigation in the survey.

2.4.2 Translating the Survey Into Spanish

Another factor that had to be dealt with was the necessity of translating the survey into Spanish for several churches whose membership included many from the Hispanic community. Providing a survey solely in English would have excluded numerous people, especially in the Catholic Church and the Mennonite Church. A former student of mine graciously agreed to attempt to translate the survey. Apparently, his translation was sufficient because no one complained about it in the "Comments" section on the back of the survey nor were there any verbal complaints to myself or the pastors at the churches concerning Spanish grammar, syntax, or vocabulary.

---

18. The terms, "Chakras," "Subtle energy," and "Ley lines," were unknown to many people.

2.4.3 Securing Responses and Response Rate

One of the most important tasks was to get the parishioners to actually partake in the survey. Several churches mentioned my project during the "Announcements" section of the morning worship time the week before my survey and continued to do so until the two-week period was over after Super Sunday. I also had the fortune of being allowed to speak to Mennonite Church members directly to ask for their assistance.[19] A few churches also mentioned my survey in their newsletter for the month of April.

The response rate was much less than anticipated, though (See Figure 1). Out of a total of 850 surveys provided before Super Sunday, the participating congregations turned in only 150. A 30 percent return was strived for; 17.6 percent was the actual overall percentage of surveys returned from the original distribution amount. This is dramatically different than the Kendal Project's response rate. According to Heelas and Woodhead, they "distributed 516 copies of the congregational domain questionnaire to the four case study churches as well as the Roman Catholic Church; 187 were completed and returned (almost entirely by post), a response rate of 36 per cent."[20]

Case Studies	Attendance at Count	Returned Survey Amount
First Presbyterian	149	35
United Methodist	152	26
St. James Catholic	920	41
First Mennonite	56	15
7th-Day Adventist	174	15
Mc Covenant Youth	18	18
Total	1469	150

Figure 1 - Congregational Attendance/Survey Return Ratio

19. This church had the highest percentage of participation with the surveys.

20. Heelas et al., *The Spiritual Revolution*, 153.

Another difference was the fact that 90 percent of the completed McMinnville surveys were turned in personally to the collection boxes; very few came through regular mail. It is impossible to know for certain why people participated or not, although Herzog and Bachman state, "Many researchers are convinced that survey instruments have a maximum length beyond which there is an increasing probability of premature termination, random responding, or other behavior patters which result in data of lower quality."[21] The surveys might have been considered too long, the project not a high priority, or perhaps considered an invasion of privacy.

2.5 Congregational Surveys: Major Similarities and Differences

Besides the congregational type differences and demographic particulars mentioned earlier for each congregational case study in the McMinnville Project, there were several facets of religiosity these groups held in common or upon which they differed. These similar/dissimilar aspects concern religious practices (both institutional and personal) as well as extra-church activities, specifically focusing on attendance, the importance of faith, and attitudes toward the holistic milieu.

Within the congregational case studies, there is a strong similarity between the churches concerning attendance. Some 90.9 percent attend once or more a week at the First Presbyterian Church, 92 percent attend once or more a week at the United Methodist Church, 95.1 percent attend once or more a week at St. James Catholic Church, and 83 percent attend once or more a week at First Mennonite Church.

Both supplemental case study groups also demonstrated high attendance commitment—all the survey participants from the Seventh Day Adventist Church said they attended once a week or more, and 88.2 percent of the McMinnville Covenant Church

21. Herzog and Bachman, "Effects of Questionnaire Length on Response Quality," 549.

Youth Group attended once a week or more. Furthermore, only an average of 8.5 percent of the congregations attended once a month or less. Attendance seems to be a priority to those attending on Super Sunday.

One of the biggest similarities within the case studies concerned spiritual activities performed at home (See Figure 3). Some 90 percent of all survey participants said they prayed at home; 75.3 percent of survey participants said they read their bibles at home. Only 12 percent of survey participants from all churches did yoga at home, a mere 3.3 percent of participants do Tai Chi at home, and just 2 percent perform or receive spiritual healing at home.

How Often Attend?	Once/Week or More	Less Than 4 Times/Year
First Presbyterian	90.9%	0.0%
United Methodist	92.3%	0.0%
St. James Catholic	95.1%	2.0%
First Mennonite	83.3%	2.0%
7th-Day Adventist	100%	0.0%
Mc Covenant Youth	88.2%	2.0%

Figure 2 - Weekly Church Attendance:
Congregational Survey Results

	Frequency (Out of 150)	Percent
Pray	135	90
Meditate	69	46
Read Bible	113	75.3
Yoga	18	12
Tai Chi	5	3.3
Spiritual Healing	3	2.0

Figure 3 - Spiritual Activities Performed at Home:
Congregational Survey Results

Another similarity revolved around participants' core beliefs about spirituality. The majority of the congregational study groups indicated that they thought that "spirituality is obeying God's will"—First Baptist Church (81.2 percent), St. James Catholic Church (46.3 percent), First Mennonite Church (78.5 percent), and the Seventh Day Adventist Church (86.6 percent). Both the United Methodist Church (34.6 percent) and the McMinnville Covenant Church Youth Group (35.2 percent) had the fewest participants stating that "spirituality is obeying God's will"; their participants' other choices were spread out fairly evenly among the options.

There was also a great similarity in what the congregations considered the highest authority in their lives (See Figure 4). In all case studies, "God" was at the top of their authority rankings. 90.6 percent of survey participants at First Presbyterian Church, 69.2 percent of participants from the United Methodist Church, 82.9 percent of participants from St. James Catholic Church, 50 percent of participants from the First Mennonite Church, 66.6 percent of participants from the Seventh Day Adventist Church, and the 41.1 percent of the youth from the McMinnville Covenant Church Youth Group said "God" was the highest authority in their lives.

All congregations (besides the First Mennonite Church) gave Scripture a significantly low authority rating—First Presbyterian Church (6.2 percent), United Methodist Church (3.8 percent), St. James Catholic Church (2.4 percent). Some 28.5 percent of the First Mennonite Church congregation gave Scripture second highest ranking. Only a few congregational survey participants (7.3 percent) from St. James Catholic Church gave "The Church" highest authority in their lives.

	Scripture	Church	God
First Presbyterian	6.2%	0.0%	90.6%
United Methodist	3.8%	0.0%	69.2%
St. James Catholic	2.4%	7.3%	82.9%
First Mennonite	25.5%	0.0%	50.0%
7th-Day Adventist	33.3%	0.0%	66.6%
Mc Covenant Youth	0.0%	5.8%	41.1%

Figure 4 - Institutional Authority in Your Life:
Congregational Survey Results

Regarding the importance of their faith, most of the congregational survey participants ranked their faith an "8" or above; however, the United Methodist Church showed the greatest dynamic of faith rankings (1 to 10, but "5" was not selected by anyone from the church). The Catholic Church also had a wider range of faith rankings, but besides two people, no one from its congregation scored lower than a "6."

One of the more divergent aspects of the congregational case studies concerned the survey participants' acceptance or rejection of alternative spirituality activities (See Figure 5). From the data, there is no set pattern of acceptance or rejection within the churches that can clearly be seen in any of their potential choices (unacceptable, unnecessary, useful, helpful, or can teach). In their responses, 21.2 percent of First Presbyterian Church participants, 15.3 percent of United Methodist Church participants, 4.8 percent of St. James Catholic Church participants, 42.8 percent of First Mennonite Church participants, 53.3 percent of Seventh Day Adventist Church participants, 5.8 percent of the McMinnville Covenant Church Youth Group indicated they thought that activities from the holistic milieu were "unacceptable."

	Unacceptable	Unnecessary	Useful	Helpful	Things to Teach
First Presbyterian	21.2	42.4	42.4	6	38.4
United Methodist	15.3	19	53.8	23	23
St. James Catholic	4.8	13.6	63.4	19.5	26.8
First Mennonite	42.8	57.1	28.5	0	7.1
7th-Day Adventist	53.3	13.3	46.6	6.6	0
Mc Covenant Youth	5.8	0	47	35.2	0

Figure 5 - Tolerance of Alternative Spirituality Activities:
Congregational Survey Results

Additionally, 42.4 percent of First Presbyterian Church participants, 19 percent of United Methodist Church participants, 13.6 percent of St. James Catholic Church participants, 57.1 percent of First Mennonite Church participants, 13.3 percent of Seventh Day Adventist Church participants, none of the McMinnville Covenant Church Youth Group indicated that they thought activities from the holistic milieu were "unnecessary."

Countering this, 42.4 percent of First Presbyterian Church participants, 53.8 percent of United Methodist Church participants, 63.4 percent of St. James Catholic Church participants, 28.5 percent of First Mennonite Church participants, 46.6 percent of Seventh Day Adventist Church participants, 47 percent of McMinnville Covenant Church indicated that they thought activities from the holistic milieu are "useful."

Furthermore, 6 percent of First Presbyterian Church participants, 23 percent of United Methodist Church participants, 19.5 percent of St. James Catholic Church participants, 6.6 percent of Seventh Day Adventist Church participants, 35.2 percent of McMinnville Covenant Church Youth Group, no First Mennonite Church participants indicated that they thought activities from the holistic milieu were "helpful"; and 38.4 percent of First Presbyterian Church participants, 23 percent of United Methodist Church participants, 26.8 percent of St. James Catholic Church participants, 7.1 percent of First Mennonite Church participants, no Seventh Day Adventist Church participants, and no McMinnville Covenant Church Youth Group participants indicated that they thought activities from the holistic milieu have "things to teach Christianity."

2.6 Investigating the Holistic Milieu

One of Heelas and Woodhead's claims in *The Spiritual Revolution* is that the traditional avenues of Christianity are being abandoned in England for the more nuanced alternative spirituality activities. They state, "We predict that in 40 or so years time the congregational domain and holistic milieu of Britain will have become much the same size."[22] This may be true in Kendal, but the notion is hard to substantiate in McMinnville considering the modicum number of holistic milieu centers.

Although it is true that two to three centers were located for the McMinnville Project, the attendance numbers of these groups[23] together did not surpass fifty participants. Furthermore, even if one enhances the number of holistic milieu practitioners to over a hundred attendees, it is still a very low ratio compared to the non-churched or churched numbers—0.002 percent compared with 1.6 percent of Kendal,[24] one hundredfold less than Kendal.

Besides the sociological significance of this (explained in chapter 6), there are several practical issues concerning the holistic milieu—how does one find, survey, or interview 50 to 100 individuals out of a city of 30,000? For, as Salganik and Heckathorn attest,

> Standard sampling and estimation techniques require the researcher to select sample members with a known probability of selection. In most cases this requirement means that researchers must have a sampling frame, a

22. Heelas et al., *The Spiritual Revolution*, 149.

23. *The Bahá'ís, The McMinnville Meditation Center, The Buddhist Contemplation Group*.

24. Heelas et al., *The Spiritual Revolution*, 40.

list of all members in the population. However, for many populations of interest such a list does not exist.[25]

Even Heelas and Woodhead agree that in their study, "The task was demanding, for it was no means easy to track down all those activities which have to do with holistic spirituality."[26] Beyond this hurdle, other issues can arise such as how to gain entrance into somewhat protective groups that have often been insulted and ridiculed by society, and how to gathering information on alternative spirituality groups if they do not want to be found or analyzed. Unfortunately, these methodological questions soon became more than rhetorical as the doors kept closing for any sociological investigations.

2.6.1 Holistic Milieu Questionnaires

The holistic milieu surveys were handled and edited very much the same way that the church surveys were dealt with earlier. Vocabulary was altered to culturally make sense to Oregonians, so, as with the congregational surveys, "Pounds" was changed to "Dollars." Furthermore, political and religious group names were changed to their American counterparts.

Some groups that had no similar corresponding group in America were simply left off the survey. Question 30 on the original Kendal holistic milieu survey was changed from "Where is Findhorn?" to "Where is the Burning Man Festival?" for relevance to American culture. The names of the alternative spirituality groups were untouched, partially to see how far these groups influence could be felt. All in all, though, the survey contents remained very much the same as in the Kendal Project.

---

25. Salganik and Heckathorn, "Sampling and Estimation in Hidden Populations Using Respondent-Driven Sampling," 194.

26. Heelas et al., *The Spiritual Revolution*, 36.

2.6.2 Mapping the Holistic Milieu

Three methods were used in an attempt to discover the holistic milieu presence in McMinnville: a public information inquiry via phone books and the Internet, a personal investigation of coffee house and library billboards that potentially exhibit holistic milieu groups and contact phone numbers, and through secondary contacts—people already involved in the holistic milieu who know people involved in the holistic milieu, etc.

Yet, before the searching began for holistic milieu groups, one of the first obstacles to overcome was defining what groups or activities exactly made up the holistic milieu in McMinnville, Oregon. Another issue dealt with concerned the names listed in various sources that might or might not be connected to the holistic milieu.

Part of the confusion lay in the structure of the holistic milieu as it "collects abundant psychological, therapeutic, magic, marginally scientific, and older esoteric material, repackages them, and offers them for individual consumption and further private syncretism."[27] Some labels, such as Astrology, Reiki or the Sai Baba Group, are typically linked with the holistic milieu; others, such as a cancer care group, chiropractice, counseling, foot massage, or Taize singing group are more loosely connected to both traditional and alternative spirituality groups.

However, it was the "private syncretism" that gives credence to the idea that radical individualism is not just a phenomenon involving the religiously churched or unchurched; this over-arching individual approach to spirituality also was part of the lives of the people active within the holistic milieu. They would often be members of several religious or spiritual groups at the same time.

One interviewee during the project, Neil, is a quintessential example. At our first meeting, he handed me a curriculum vitae of his different religious/spirituality honors and titles. It showed that his spirituality engulfed a number of faiths and spiritual movements—some traditional, some alternative, but all mystical and

---

27. Luckman, "The Privatisation of Religion and Morality," 75.

transcendent. His spiritual life was like a web; it was "diaphanous like the spiritualities of Alternative and New Age seekers and its spiral form affirms the creative self-reflective process of the central web-maker."[28]

Neil had holistic milieu knowledge and contacts, and he was very willing to help. He suggested to me the possibility of distributing some surveys at *The New Thought* gathering in McMinnville. Neil wrote to me in an email, "My plan is to contact a McMinnville friend who is a member of two (2) spiritual groups and ask for an entree to present your questionnaire."[29] Neil was quite helpful, and his additional footwork for the project was greatly appreciated.

Utilizing the telephone Yellow Pages® provided a short list compiled of three to four potential holistic milieu centers based on the same group types in Kendal. The next step was to investigate any Internet offerings or listings for possible holistic milieu groups, but this provided little to go on and was unreliable.

Eventually, a handful of groups were contacted and/or a voice message left on their recorders, but only one ever called back—the Baháʾí Center. As Dandelion puts it, "Democratic gatekeeping can be complicated, and is also time-consuming."[30] He should have added, " . . . and not always guaranteed."

2.6.3 The Sample

The Baháʾí Center leader, Delane, was very amiable and accommodating at first to the notion of taking part of the survey and project. She asked to read the survey ahead of time and, once she received via email, spoke to her group about the possibility. Unfortunately, they replied, "The survey instrument was an inadequate tool for responding. Often, the terms needed redefining or clarifying. Also,

---

28. Corrywright, "Network Spirituality: The Schumacher-Resurgence-Kumar Nexus," 315.

29. Neil, holistic milieu participant, email message to author (January 20, 2007).

30. Dandelion, *A Sociology Analysis of the Theology of Quakers*, 52.

to classify world religions (Buddhist, Baháʼí) as groups in amongst therapies, 'support groups' is inappropriate in our view."[31]

More disappointment came when *The New Thought* leadership replied to Neil, "I read through it and my feeling at this time is that it is a great study that he is doing but I doubt that we would want to participate at this time." This is definitely one limitation to the snowball sampling technique,[32] which depends upon referrals from initial contacts to find and bring in additional participants. There are so many social variables in play between people that any number of circumstances surrounding Neil might have closed the gate, potentially.

The holistic milieu surveys were distributed, filled out, and collected, but the number was small (nine). It was a "spider-web" affair in that most people who took the survey had heard about it from another individual they were connected with in their spiritual journey.

The interviewees lived all around McMinnville or just outside of the city (but within five miles). Nevertheless, it was a problematical endeavour although there was significance in the responses of the rejecting holistic milieu practitioners. Their responses showed a wariness of organized religious and spiritual scrutiny that they considered potentially injurious to their harmony and possible survival as a group.

2.6.4 Holistic Milieu Survey Distribution and Collection

For the holistic milieu surveys, the most advantageous method of disbursement was simply to email a copy to the participants who asked for them. However, Neil distributed twenty surveys to holistic milieu people he knew within McMinnville. A small number of people asked for the survey to be emailed to them, and later completed it, mailing it back to me via regular postal mail. A few people handed me their surveys in person, four people mailed them back

---

31. Delane, Baháʼí leader, email message to author (April 18, 2007).

32. Aldridge and Levine, *Surveying the Social World*, 80.

to me several weeks after receiving them, two people asked for an emailed copy to return to me later with the answers either bolded or checked off, and Neil handed some to me, personally.

Even though the quantity was not as overflowing as with the congregational case studies, the information gathered still showed clear Sacro-Egoistical and Sacro-Communal traits in their responses.

2.7 The Interviews

Interviews were undertaken to discern the depth and private reality of Sacro-Egoism in McMinnville. Whereas the church surveys gave a wider view of Christianity in Oregon, the interviews provided a deep gaze into what people believe about Christianity in McMinnville, what role it plays in their everyday lives, and to test the traits of Sacro-Egoism in McMinnville society.

Time and location were carefully selected to help the interviewees feel comfortable about discussing what most people consider highly confidential information. Most of the time, the interviewee ultimately decided the meeting spots and appointment times. These meeting sites ranged from personal homes to coffee houses to restaurants to churches to sidewalk tables outside of a bistro restaurant. All interviewees were informed that the meetings would probably last anywhere from one to two hours in duration.

The meetings began with typical salutations and introductions, a brief description of the interview expectations were presented, and the interviewees were allowed to ask any questions they might have about the project before the interview continued. The question period of the interview was varied, but not without purpose or direction. The interviewees were allowed to ruminate and elucidate as long as they wanted on the questions (which no one voiced any objection to). If the interviewee seemed unsure on how to respond, another more defining question would be offered or the question would be skipped until later in the process.

The questions, of course, revolved around topics relevant to the key findings of the survey results, traditional Christianity, and the holistic milieu. Generally, six main questions were provided with subsequent detailed inquiries, if necessary: 1) What sort of religious upbringing or experiences do you have?, 2) What do you think of institutional religion, specifically Christianity?, 3) What aspect of church life do you find attractive and why?, 4) Where do you see the church heading in the future?, 5) What do you think of alternative avenues of spirituality, specifically non-traditional ones?, and 6) "What has the highest spiritual or religious authority in your life?"

No resistance or offense was given by the interviewees to these questions; rather, they seemed eager to speak their minds.

2.7.1 The Interview Sample

It was decided that an interview with two candidates from each church and category in the McMinnville study should be arranged—preferably representing both genders. Thus, people who had indicated on their surveys that they would be willing to be interviewed were contacted from St. James Catholic Church, First Presbyterian Church, United Methodist Church, First Mennonite Church, and two from the holistic milieu. Supplementally, two teenagers, who had earlier participated in the youth survey at the McMinnville Covenant Church, also agreed to be interviewed.

In the end, eleven people agreed to be interviewed. Some of their names were obtained from the surveys; some of the names were provided by the pastors as good candidates. Everyone who agreed to be interviewed in the congregational study had participated in the survey. Only the holistic milieu potential interview names were attained from others.

2.8 Street Survey

In an attempt to further define the religiosity framework representative of all of McMinnville, especially those people not overtly associated with a church or denomination, a street survey was undertaken on Sunday, October 22, 2006. On that day, volunteers stopped at one hundred and seventy-five houses with the intention of administering a short, eighteen-question survey that would help reveal the religious and spiritual beliefs of those not demonstratively attending at either traditional or alternative spirituality centers.

2.8.1 Street Survey Location Choice

A central location in McMinnville was chosen with a diverse housing makeup consisting of ranch-style homes, duplexes, and trailer homes. This 450 x 400 meter block area was situated two blocks from the main thoroughfare in McMinnville and had a school, a few churches, and a fire station nearby. There was a 100-unit apartment complex, but it was not surveyed (sadly) because of the honoring of a posted, "No Solicitors" sign. Overall, this area contained over one hundred possible homes and residences to be surveyed, which is comparable to the number of houses (116) potentially available in the Kendal Project.[33]

2.8.2 Pre-Street Survey Preparations

The residents of the potential survey area had received door hangers the week before indicating the McMinnville Project name, the purposes of the survey, the volunteer identity of the survey takers, and the general time frame of the door-to-door interviews. Door hangers were distributed because alone it would have taken me too long to knock on each door, hand the occupants a flyer, and explain what was going to occur on the survey day. Moreover, it was an innocuous and non-threatening way to get the message out.

33. "Street Survey Findings," *The Kendal Project*; online: http://www.lancs.ac.uk/fss/projects/ieppp/kendal/streetsurveyfindings.htm.

A team of helpers was organized, chosen, and cultivated from the Super Sunday volunteer list; these were the people who were considered to be the most reliable, outgoing, friendly, and who demonstrated good communication skills. The volunteers were given great latitude in their presentation of the surveys in the hopes that more participants would open up and honestly divulge their feelings and beliefs on the complicated and controversial topic of religion.

2.8.3 Street Survey Design

Unlike the Super Sunday surveys, which were designed to delve deep into the religious practices of its participants, the Street Survey surveys were meant to be as concise, clear, and very brief. It is not an overstatement to say that people dislike door-to-door salespeople, missionaries, fund-raisers, etc. Thus, the main goal behind the design of the Street Survey was to encourage participation without fear of over-commitment, and yet, that the survey would still ask valuable questions that would provide a reliable and valid sounding of the participants' understanding and beliefs of religiosity and spirituality.

The survey was reduced to two pages with appropriate spots for the participants' first names and their addresses. It included eighteen questions on both the participants' traditional and alternative spirituality habits/activities as well as questions regarding their religious beliefs on the existence of God, the afterlife, and spiritual power.

2.8.4 Implementing the Street Survey

The day of the Street Survey was "blessed" with beautiful sunny weather, which is unusual for Oregon in October, which normally receives 2.67" of rain during that month.[34] Maps were distributed,

---

34. "Weather," online: http://www.travelportland.com/visitors/weather. html.

volunteers were paired up to tackle assigned streets and sides (and for safety), and cell phone numbers were shared to ensure that any questions could be immediately answered.

Not knowing for certain how long the entire survey would take, a minimum path of homes was established for the volunteers to follow for the survey to have merit; however, as the students quickly and expediently interviewed and completed their surveys, more homes were added, finishing the "optimum plan." The whole affair took only two and a half hours and, in the end, 175 homes were approached. Of those 175 homes, forty-five people agreed to be interviewed, nineteen refused, and no one was home or answered at the remaining 111 homes.

The nineteen people who declined to be interviewed did provide some informative reasons behind their refusals to participate. The vast majority of reasons was personal in nature and not based on any theological or atheistic grounds. Even though these people refused to take part in the survey, only one or two were harsh or hostile in their responses to the volunteers.

Of those that agreed to be interviewed, most seemed happy to oblige although one man demanded the volunteer, "Make it quick." In another peculiar instance, one couple refused to be interviewed, but insisted their children take the survey. One person first refused, but upon reflection and some assurances by the volunteer, agreed to take the survey.

As with the Super Sunday volunteers, the Street Survey volunteers were excited and positive about their time in the field and were eager to share their stories when we met to gather the surveys. Everyone seemed relatively energized by the event; most said the people they encountered were more open than they had predicted.

2.8.5 Street Survey Milieu

In the Street Survey, twenty-four people indicated that they were currently attending church in McMinnville (See Figure 6). Within these twenty-four, at least one person claimed association with the following churches: Abundant Life Pentecost, Calvary Chapel,

McMinnville Covenant Church, Family Bible Fellowship, First Christian Church, LDS, McMinnville Christian Faith Center, New Horizons, Seventh Day Adventist, United Methodist Church, and an undisclosed non-denominational church. Of the remaining people who claimed church attendance, Bethel Baptist Church had the largest numbers of participants in the Street Survey (five), followed by St. James Catholic Church (four), and the Church on the Hill (three).

Do You Attend Church?	Frequency	Percent
Yes	24	53.3
No	20	44.4
No Answer	1	2.2
Total	45	100

Figure 6 - Street Survey Church Attendance
Street Survey Results

For these active participants attending a local church, their engagement with religious organizations was crucial in their personal lives. This is evident from the survey data. When asked to rate the importance of their spiritual lives, the majority (thirty-eight people) said their spiritual life was "very or pretty important." Only six people said it was of "somewhat or no importance." Beyond this, 45 percent of the participants admitted to being involved in some sort of extra-church activity, from "prayer" to "missions trips" to "Bible study" to "church softball."

Twenty people in the Street Survey mentioned that they had once gone to church, but had stopped for a variety of reasons. Only three gave reasons remotely connected to criticism of the institution of the church. One person said they stopped because of "thirteen years of Catholic school," another said that they were "still looking for a new church," and one said they stopped but "went as they were growing up." All other reasons were of a personal or secular nature.

2.8.6 *Street Survey Extra-Church Activities*

Of the twenty-three in the Street Survey who said they attended church regularly, fourteen said they did participate in spiritual activities outside their church. Eight mentioned to the volunteers that they prayed, ten said they read the Bible or were involved in a Bible study, one person said he was signed up with a softball team sponsored by the church, one person said she was involved in Child Evangelism Fellowship, one person said he belonged to a Masonic Lodge, one person said he was attending a drug and alcohol faith-based rehabilitation program, and another said she was involved with a Home School Cooperative program. Besides, perhaps, the one individual involved in the Masonic lodge, no one else mentioned any alternative spirituality practices associated with the holistic milieu.

2.9 Reflections on the McMinnville Project

The McMinnville Project, as with the Kendal Project, was an extreme effort of planning, implementation, and analysis. Overall, the McMinnville Project experience was positive and academically beneficial because it opened a door into the inner beliefs and activities of average citizens regarding a controversial topic of study and conversation. An old American axiom states, "Do not talk about religion or politics" (unless one wants to get into an argument), but this project aimed to do exactly that—to probe people for their sincere beliefs about religion, the Church, and the holistic milieu.

The more serious side of the project included the lead up and orchestration of the details of making this project work. Despite these complications, the chores and responsibilities required for such an undertaking were sufficiently managed. Yearly checklists were devised of tasks and their deadlines to help keep the Project running on time. Such strategic thinking kept wasted effort at a minimum and ensured a timely conclusion to the Project.

Borrowing the survey structure from the Kendal Project (with their permission) was both beneficial and detracting. It was helpful because it avoided the awesome job of thinking up the questions and remaking the wheel, so to speak. As a sociological study, the survey was comprehensive and the questions on target for what they sought to ascertain.

There were some issues about the word choice, length, and layout of the survey raised by those who took the survey (and me). Many questions were irrelevant to direct religious investigation and were questioned or ignored by the participants. More than once, the words, "None of your business," were written in near questions relating to politics and economics. Additionally, the length of the surveys was substantial. Filling out the survey took some time, effort, and depth of thought—a factor affecting involvement in this study, but in analysis of the data gathered, a powerful machine of sociological forces was clearly perceivable.

The following chapter discusses the "gears" of religious reality in motion in McMinnville and conceivably the entire Western world, currently.

—— 3 ——

Church Life in the West

3.0 Introduction

DESPITE THE FACT THAT only 21 percent of McMinnville citizens attended church on Super Sunday, church life is still a priority to thousands of the city's inhabitants, based on statistical and investigational data gathered for this thesis. During the McMinnville Project, nearly every church was scientifically observed at least one time during the project and several congregations permitted deeper sociological analysis through the distribution of surveys to their members and interviews of key examples within the survey groups. The amount of data retrieved was immense and, extremely informative regarding worship trends, beliefs, and future patterns of adherence or abandonment of religiosity.

The central part of this chapter expands upon the manifestation of Sacro-Egoism with regards to the church life in McMinnville. It establishes the reality of Sacro-Egoism by connecting the definitional characteristics of self-authority with four other key components identified through the research: a personal commitment to spirituality, a personal commitment to Jesus, a personal investment in the Bible, and a tolerant attitude toward extra-church activities/beliefs.

The manifestation and relationship of the Sacro-States within the Congregational studies is then examined. It compares the survey data for connections to and manifestations of the three Sacro-State expressions of Sacro-Clericalism, Sacro-Communalism, and Sacro-Theism. It also addresses some fundamental issues about investigating and forming conclusions on their influence and existence in McMinnville society.

3.1 Sacro-Egoism in the McMinnville Study

When one examines the answers of the survey participants and the responses of the case study interviewees in the McMinnville Project, important patterns emerge about what religiosity and spirituality mean to these citizens of McMinnville. Individual authority, the original defining characteristic of Sacro-Egoism, was found to be complemented by four other dominant indicators—a personal commitment to spirituality, a personal commitment to Jesus, a personal investment in the Bible, and a tolerant attitude toward extra-church activities and beliefs. Each is examined below in turn.

3.1.1 Sources of Authority

Both the surveys and the interviews showed clear patterns of what the modern believer/spiritual being insisted upon within their religious environment. The notional characteristic of Sacro-Egoism—i.e., that people consider their own spiritual/religious understandings to be of the highest authority in life, was found to be highly developed in this sample. Furseth and Repstad state, "The individual's own feelings constitute the criterion for truth, not an external religious authority."[1]

Other authorities such as the pastor, church body, or the Bible may be granted some power, but ultimately, it is the individual's idea of religious right or wrong that has the final authority. As Hunt suggests,

---

1. Furseth and Repstad, *An Introduction to the Sociology of Religion*, 122.

> In terms of secularization, it would seem to follow that it is the "religious"—that is, reference to the supernatural and its organizational expressions—which is in the decline, but that it is the "sacred," which endures, indeed is transformed within the contemporary setting.[2]

This individual authoritarianism has become evident in all denominations and possibly in many faiths. When asked in the congregational survey about their core beliefs regarding spirituality, not one person chose the option, "Spirituality is overcoming the ego." Clearly, the individual ego is embraced in McMinnville and not considered a threat or obstacle to spirituality. Instead, it holds the key to their approach to church life or religiosity. This can be further observed in both other survey responses and the congregational interviews.

Within the congregational survey data, the diminishing role of the church institution is evident. As Furseth and Repstad further state, "Religion practiced by the large majority of people in the West tends to be critical of tradition, critical of authority, subjective, eclectic, and focused on identity and self-realization."[3] Miller's summation of institutionalism substantiates this concept: "I suppose we need them. The institutions. The corporations. But mostly I don't like them. I don't have to like them either. It's my right."[4]

Thus, presented with the question, "Which of these would you say is the highest authority in your life?," only 2.7 percent of the congregational survey respondents claimed, "The Church." Furthermore, only 8.7 percent claimed "Scripture" as being the highest authority in their life. However, 6.7 percent claimed that "Your own reason or judgment" was the highest and 6.7 percent claimed that "Your intuition or feelings" had the highest authority in their lives (See Figure 7). Clearly, in balance, churchgoers in McMinnville hold themselves as higher sources of authority than the church and the Bible.

2. Hunt, *Religion and Everyday Life*, 169.

3. Furseth and Repstad, *An Introduction to the Sociology of Religion*, 124.

4. Miller, *Blue Like Jazz*, 130.

	Frequency	Percent
Scripture	13	8.7
The Church	4	2.6
God	105	70.0
Your Own Reason or Judgment	10	6.7
Your Intuition or Feelings	10	6.7
More Than One	3	2.0
Blank	1	0.7
Total	146	97.5
Missing	4	2.6
Total	150	100.0

Figure 7 - Highest Authority in Your Life:
Congregational Survey Results

Regarding changing patterns of authority in Catholicism, Hoge remarks, "Generally, young Catholics had a vision of Catholicism which included less church authority and less rigid boundaries than was the case of older Catholics."[5] He continues, "Young Catholics feel that they live in a culture of choice and are entitled to make choices."[6] This soft approach to Catholicism downplays the institution of the Catholic Church, but upholds the community of Catholics, both internationally and locally.

In her interview, Joyce (St. James Catholic Church member) said, "I take a piece from this church (say, meditation) and a piece from another (like Social Justice) and combine them." Linda, the second Catholic interviewee, responded in similar fashion. She stated, "There is some authority from being a Catholic, but not as much as there used to be. The Northwest is definitely a different place because they insist that they are independent, eco-minded, but I just see a lot of self-centeredness."

5. Hoge, "Core and Periphery in American Catholic Identity," 301.

6. Ibid., 295.

The Church institution, for these Catholics, is not necessarily the final center of religious authority. In this matter, Kennedy states, "American Catholicism, meanwhile, longs for some freedom from the absolute rejection of even discussing such issues [ordaining homosexuals or women to the priesthood] by an authoritarian bureaucracy that tends to emphasize control and conformity."[7] Hoge concludes, "It follows that Catholic teaching, especially to the young, . . . needs to avoid negative appeals to obligation, duty, or guilt."[8]

This notion is not just a Catholic trend. In a supplemental interview with Tammy, a McMinnville resident and Quaker who worships in the local city of Newberg, she blatantly stated, "Jesus came to abolish institutional religion. There can be good things, but since what Jesus taught was different than institutionalism, it runs contrary to the Church's teaching." She continued, "There is danger in having a head pastor because people can put too much stock in what he says. I prefer the Quietist meetings[9] because they are non-hierarchical." Another supplemental Quaker interviewee, Elizabeth, said, "The real Church is more about the community than about the morning service." For both of these women, the church structure was a means to an end of serving others, but it was not necessarily the best avenue of service for them.

This anti-institutional inclination can be seen in the interviews from other churches in McMinnville. Interviewee Esther wrote, "The American church needs a revival in the sense that they have become political more that religious." First Presbyterian Church interviewee, Ben, stated, "I think the ice cube is melting. Church folk have to join together. The church should be affirming and aware of God's intent for the church but we get stuck in the

---

7. Kennedy, "Disorganized Religion: The Episcopal and Roman Catholic Church Adopt Different Tactics for Same Problem," 20.

8. Hoge, "Core and Periphery in American Catholic Identity," 301.

9. In their view [the Quietists], man, in order to be perfect, must attain complete passivity and annihilation of the will, abandoning himself to God to such an extent that he cares neither for Heaven nor Hell, no for his own salvation. See Cross and Livingstone, eds., "Quietism," 1357.

form of the church. We don't hear what the spirit is saying. It is a scandal that the church is so fractured."

The first UMC interviewee, Joan, said, "It is not about the institution, it is a personal journey." The second interviewee, Susan, also commented, "Control is a bad part of the institutional structure. The structure tends to shift one away from Christ, but the structure also helps keep the group together."

Even the United Methodist Church pastor was advocating for this understanding of modern religious life. He offered, "Even those of us whose spiritual temperament requires a community of encouragement and support are forced to select the community ourselves, and therefore we are likely to select a community that reinforces our personal religious convictions."

The McMinnville Covenant Church Youth Group definitely demonstrated an anti-authoritarian bent in their survey responses and interview answers. As with the other churches, when asked on the survey, the Youth Group respondents said that "God" had the highest authority (38.9 percent), then "Your intuition or feelings" (27.8 percent), then "Your own reason or judgment" (22.2 percent), and then the church. Doyle notes,

> Many young people are hesitant to assent to a self-limiting creed, first, because they don't want to compromise their integrity or their authenticity by committing themselves to what is not objectively verifiable; and second, because they don't want to seem dogmatic, rigid, or intolerant.[10]

This is observable in the multitudinous new groups sprouting up that offer alternative and inviting programs for young people to attend that are not directly religious. They are fun, safe-havens that could open up into a spiritual opportunity if the students so desire.

Spiritually-minded people in McMinnville all share a common attitude that diminishes the role of the institutional Church and elevates the power of the individual. They insist that "Social and political institutions exist to serve the human person."[11]

10. Doyle, "Young Catholics & Their Faith," 12.

11. Grasso, "Christianity, Enlightenment Liberalism, and the Quest for

Churches exist for the benefit and service of the individual, not vice versa. Moreover, Shibley states, "Because Northwesterners are less tied to traditional religion, they are freer to explore alternative spirituality and more available for recruitment by new religions."[12] This attitude was evident in all denominations and even within the holistic milieu. Yet, just because people were at liberty to dabble outside of traditional boundaries, it does not mean they actually exercise that freedom.

3.1.2 Personal Commitment to Spirituality

Even though the modern believer (or spiritual seeker) is generally anti-institutional, he or she is not necessarily antinomian or atheistic. Christian Smith states, "The belief content of the Christian faith gives rise to certain practices and experiences—particular emotional ones—that many people find highly engaging, compelling, persuasive, and convincing."[13]

Additionally, Voas claims,

> Many people remain interested in church weddings and funerals, Christmas services and local festivals. They believe in "something out there," pay at least lip service to Christian values, and may be willing to identify with a denomination. They are neither regular churchgoers (now only a small minority of the population in most European countries) nor self-consciously nonreligious. Because they retain some loyalty to tradition, though in a rather uncommitted way, we can call the phenomenon fuzzy fidelity.[14]

Unlike the "Fuzzy Christianity" Voas claims to be existent in Europe, the data suggests that the Christians and seekers in McMinnville actually care about their beliefs and expressions of

---

Freedom," 303.

12. Shibley, "Secular But Spiritual in the Pacific Northwest," 140.

13. Smith, "Why Christianity Works: An Emotions-Focused Phenomenological Account," 167.

14. Voas, "The Rise and Fall of Fuzzy Fidelity in Europe," 10.

spirituality. As Furseth and Repstad remark, people " . . . seek a religious community on a regular basis and that this participation is important to them."[15] Furthermore, Roof claims, "It's not that community has been abandoned in our highly individualistic, therapeutic culture so much as new forms of community have arisen, organized around personal concerns and feelings."[16]

This notion is backed up in the data from the McMinnville study. In the congregational survey, when asked, "If you had to rank the importance of your faith from 1 to 10, where 1 indicates it is completely insignificant and 10 indicates it is the most important thing in your life, what number would you give?," 43.3 percent of individuals ranked their faiths as "10," Another 16.7 percent of respondents ranked their faith as a "9," and 18.7 percent ranked their faith as an "8." Only 14.1 percent of people together tolled ranked the importance of the faith as "1–7."

Of the church-going participants in the Street Survey, when asked, "How important is the spiritual side of life to you?" (See Figure 8), 84.4 percent indicated they felt their faith was "Very important" or "Pretty important" combined. Only 13.3 percent indicated, "Somewhat or Not at all." Pointing to ulterior prioritization, a small percentage (6.7 percent) indicated that they held "finding happiness" in life as their highest importance. A lesser percentage yet indicated that they were not concerned with spirituality (2 percent) nor did they believe in it (0.7 percent).

15. Furseth and Repstad, An Introduction to the Sociology of Religion, 130.

16. Roof, "God is in the Details: Reflections on Religion's Public Presence in the United States in the Mid 1990's," 157.

	Frequency	Percent
Not At All	1	2.2
Somewhat	5	11.2
Pretty Important	11	24.4
Very Important	27	60
No Answer	1	2.2
Total	45	100

Figure 8 - Importance of Spiritual Life:
Street Survey Results

The personal concern for their spirituality is evident in the congregational survey responses when asked if they had stopped going to church, but had started up again. Explaining their choice of participation, one person wrote in, "I missed closeness with God." Others wrote, "I reached the end of myself and had no where to go but to God;" "I missed feeling good with God," "God erased the emotional hurt;" "The futility of life without God;" "I missed going;" "Personal calling from God;" and "experiencing God's love."

Interviewee Esther stated of her time in church, "I enjoy the quiet, reflective times of devotions . . . that sense of inner peace and purpose." Ben (FPC) remarked, "God and I took a walk and God did most of the talking and I went back the next fall and changed my major to pastoral ministry."

One can see this personal concern in the attendance data from both the congregational survey and the Street Survey. Most respondents in the congregational survey showed a strong commitment to their churches in the form of attendance. When asked, "Do you go to church regularly," 32.3 percent said that they did. When pressed further, 38 percent indicated they attended church "More than once a week," 50.7 percent said they attended "Once a week," and only 2 percent said they attended "Less than four times a year, at least once a year."

In the Street Survey, of the participants who indicated they attended church, 38 percent said they attended "More than once a week," 42.8 percent said they attended "Once a week," and no one indicated that they attended "Less than once a month" (See Figure 9).

How Often Attend Church?	Frequency	Percent
More Than Once/Week	9	20.0
Once/Week	9	20.0
Every 2 Weeks	4	8.9
Once/Month	1	2.2
Less Than Once/Month	2	4.4
No Answer	17	37.8

Figure 9 - Street Survey Church Frequency
of Attendance: Street Survey Results

The participants of the Street Survey do have personal religious standards that they insist upon being maintained to protect their individual spirituality. Some of these standards are entrusted with key people within the church; others are outside of the church structure or community, but "Individuals in emerging churches participate in a spirituality that integrates the corporate and the personal."[17]

3.1.3 Personal Commitment to Jesus

An interesting characteristic (especially considering the Spiritual Revolution's contention that people are embracing non-traditional spiritual elements) observed in both the surveys and the interviews was the fixture of Jesus and the Bible in people's lives. In the congregational surveys, when asked, "Which of the following would you say is most important to you?," 36 percent of respondents marked,

17. Gibbs and Bolger, *Emerging Churches*, 230.

"Deepening my relationship with Christ." Also, when asked, "Do you believe in any of the following?," 90 percent of respondents indicated that they believed that Jesus was the son of God.

One person marked down that he had started going to church again as an adult because of his "Love for Jesus and His body [the Church]"; another person wrote that he was attending because he "Loves Jesus." One person said she was attending because she was a "born again Christian"; another said, "I accepted Christ in 1999 as an adult"; and one said she was attending because she "Came to a personal, Bible-centered relationship with Jesus Christ." In the Street Survey, one participant added at the end of the interview, "I am a big believer in the Lord and the importance of faith."

Moreover, from the most conservative interviewee to the most liberal, several interviewees made mention of the personal importance and value of Jesus Christ in the way they worshipped, communed with God/the Central Force in the Universe, and related to others. Ben (FPC) remarked, "I am hopelessly committed to the scandal of the exclusivity of Jesus." Joan (UMC), stated, "I see the Church dogma for what it is. However, if I see the true love of Jesus, I stay." She explained that in her work at the church, her "main job is to teach them about Jesus." Susan (UMC), said, "It [church life] is all about serving others, like Jesus." Elizabeth (Quaker) mentioned, "To be *good*, churches need to focus on Christ." Esther (FMC) stated, "The [church] alignment with political factions is taking the focus off of the message of Christ." They may be down on the institution of the church, but they are not critical of its founder, Jesus.

Gibbs and Bolger provide the "post-mod'" understanding of Jesus for "emerging" Christians today. They state,

> Popularly, the term emerging church has been applied to high-profile, youth-oriented congregations that have gained attention on account of their rapid numerical growth; their ability to attract (or retain) twentysome-things; their contemporary worship, which draws from popular music styles; and their ability to promote

themselves to the Christian subculture through websites and by word of mouth.[18]

Emerging churches are just not about appearance, however. Additionally, they write, "The kingdom is present wherever Jesus is present. Each person experiences the kingdom through God's invitation, healing, and restoration."[19]

It is this omni-relevance to all the different Sacro approaches that keeps Jesus relevant and integral despite one's approach to religiosity. He was anti-institutional when the Jewish leaders were oppressive (Sacro-Egoism), he frequently sojourned to get right with God (Sacro-Egoism), he had several theophanies wherein God directly revealed himself to him (Sacro-Theism), he openly and magnanimously shared the good God-stuff with the marginalized and the empowered (Sacro-Communalism), and he did not come to destroy the law, but to fulfill it (Sacro-Clericalism). Jesus did not take an either/or approach to his religion or spirituality; rather, it was a holistic integration of all four approaches to spirituality.

3.1.4 Personal Investment in the Bible

The data gathered on the use and understanding of the Bible showed very interesting results. Even though most people in their survey responses did not rate Scripture highly in matters of authority, they still read it regularly, which demonstrates its personal value to them. In the congregational survey, when asked, "Do you ever do any of the following at home?," 75.3 percent of respondents marked that they read their Bible at home. Furthermore, in the Street Survey, 26 percent of respondents mentioned reading or studying the Bible when asked about alternative church activities in their lives. According to the survey data, reading the Bible is definitely an important aspect of their worship life; however, the interpretation of the Bible's contents and significance is left up to the individual.

18. Ibid., 41.
19. Ibid., 54.

Many people in the interview sessions also commented on the Bible's influence in their lives, albeit with more discretion. According to Gibbs and Bolger, people are " . . . looking to the Bible afresh without the presuppositions and restricted vision of modernity. For them, the Bible presents a fascinating collection of stories that together make up a big story that stretches from before creation to beyond the end of time."[20]

Linda (SJCC) stated, "I get my authority from the Bible and my understanding of what is right and just. In fact, the Bible supercedes the priest's authority." Joyce (SJCC) described her typical approach to spiritual questions this way: "I first seek in the Bible, then I talk to wise Christians (a smattering) from different sides –liberal and conservative, but my husband has the final say on moral matters or major decisions." Susan (UMC) expands the understanding of the role of the Bible in her life. She says, "We study the Bible in a small inter-faith group. We seek its relevancy—What does it mean to me? Why should I care about that? The Bible is not a scientific document; it is the story of people." Ben (FPC) stated, "It is a creative tension between the community of faith, Scripture, and the Spirit." As Ballard remarks, these people give evidence that the Bible " . . . is authoritative and normative but, within a wider context of faith, constantly rediscovered and reinterpreted."[21] The church's position on the Bible is not as important as their personal view and interpretation of it.

Of course, there are inherent dangers with this attitude. As Holland remarks, "The present individualistic reading of Scripture, which has largely lost the corporate dimension of the early church's mindset, has promoted an individualism that has sometimes been unbiblical, unhealthy and dangerously divisive."[22] Many in the church also see a watering-down of core, foundational truths. Father Baron suggests, "The result of this privatization is a political and cultural arena stripped of religious values and insights."[23]

20. Ibid., 70.

21. Ballard, "The Scriptures in Church and Pastoral Practice," 41.

22. Holland, "Individualism and the People of God," 90.

23. Barron, "Not Just Lip Service," 16.

The data collected from the surveys and congregational and holistic milieu interviews points to a very personal approach to spirituality and the Bible. Rather than being "fuzzy," these people are so attuned to their own personal religious needs that the traditional trappings of religious life are superficial to them and even oppressive. As interviewee Esther mentioned, "God is the highest spiritual authority. I was formed by him for a purpose in this world. My job is to walk with Him to fulfill that purpose."

They are seeking a personal journey that is relevant and purposeful. They want to be on the "correct path." As Roof says about reality and religiosity in Los Angeles (but it is relevant to people in McMinnville, too), "If God is in the details, then for people in this city this has something to do with finding and affirming that meaningful and sustainable life."[24]

3.1.5 Openness and Toleration of Non-traditional Beliefs and Practices

Part of the dominant approach was that of determining one's own mind when it comes to religious and spiritual tenets. Wuthnow remarks, "If traditional creeds and doctrines are eroding, this trend would suggest that people might think more about meaning and purpose in the future because they would not already have ready-made answers available to them."[25] For the believers surveyed here, the church does not decide religious matters, the community does not force adherence to cultural norms, but the individual decides the path he will take. This means that the individual must be able to investigate and experience a wide variety of religious and spiritual expressions, some of which lay outside the boundaries of traditional or conventional religion.

Once a person has tried a religion (or at least considered it), then she can choose to integrate it into her life or not. Thus, a push for theological and spiritual freedom is sponsored and even

24. Roof, "God is in the Details: Reflections on Religion's Public Presence in the United States in the Mid-1990s," 158.

25. Wuthnow, *Christianity in the 21st Century*, 102.

cultivated. As Aldridge states, "The modern era is the true age of faith, where people participate in religion because they freely choose to do so."[26]

Freedom over oppression is integral to most people's religiosity as demonstrated in the survey. This is most easily seen in the congregational surveys under Question 19 of the congregational survey and in the interviews, which basically questions people's approval of alternative spirituality practices.

When asked of her view of non-traditional avenues of spirituality, interviewee Esther (FMC) responded,

> Some of these avenues can be incorporated into my own religious life. I met a Native American pastor who has successfully incorporated some of the spiritual practices from their heritage into Christian worship. Look what we have done with the winter celebrations by making them into Christmas. Did we not borrow from the pagans?

The results from the survey are also compelling. The answers from Question 19 show that 74.7 percent of the survey participants have a positive, or at least optimistic, view of holistic milieu activities. Yet, despite their affirmation, most survey participants did not find spiritual sustenance in these activities. As Ben (FPC) stated, "New Age activities are just man-made attempts to encounter the transcendent."

3.2 The Presence of Other Sacro-States

The congregational survey results point to a significant actuality in the religious and spiritual community in McMinnville, too. Although Sacro-Egoism is evident in many of the respondents' answers, there are just not Sacro-Egoists out there. The three other Sacro-States are represented, to varying degrees.

The responses from the question regarding the prioritization of Scripture and the church over one's own reason and intuition attest that 11.6 percent of survey takers may be Sacro-Clerical.

26. Aldridge, *Religion in the Contemporary World*, 100.

Another question, which asks if respondents are involved in other activities at their church, showed that more than 68 percent of the people were participating in a variety of smaller, church-related groups—a possible expression of Sacro-Communalism. Plus, looking at the survey responses to whether they believed in the power of prayer, presumably to God, 87.3 percent said they did believe in it and 90 percent of respondents said they prayed at home—another possible link to Sacro-Theism.

Beyond these figures, it is very likely that some people may exercise a mix of the Sacro-States in their understanding and appreciation to religion and spirituality. They may be Sacro-Egoistical when it comes to the Bible version they read, but Sacro-Clerical when it comes to their belief on the Sacraments. They may be Sacro-Theistic and frequently hear the voice of God by themselves as they pray, but they still perceive a need to continue their fellowship with other believers at church. They may be born into a Sacro-Communal lifestyle (due to the biological limitations of being an infant and child), but then shift into radical Sacro-Communalism when they go away to college and join a commune.

What is clear is that the Sacro-States are not static approaches—they are apt to change because people change in their perspectives and needs in life. One's freedom quotient rises exponentially in life as one gets older. Some people clearly act upon this freedom to shirk the bonds between them and the church; others cling dearly to the church as an old, trusted, valuable friend. They may not feel a need for God or church for a long time, but circumstances can change drastically and dramatically.[27]

Furthermore, parenting styles may have a huge influence on the Sacro-States. Fotana states,

> Individuals who were indulged by parents in early childhood, with signs of need such as crying automatically eliciting nurturing responses, predominantly think of God as someone whose help is contingent upon active solicitation. . . . if parental nurturing was given without

27. See "Paris Hilton: God Has Given Me This New Chance;" online: http://www.foxnews.com/story/0,2933,280415,00.html.

the need for solicitation, the individual comes to see divine help as requiring neither ritual nor obedience.[28]

Zohar and Marshall assert (sounding somewhat Sacro-Egoistical), "The spiritually intelligent person does not simply impose his own values and expectations on his child. The spiritually intelligent parent offers a space, a nurturing soil, in which his child can grow beyond his parents and even beyond himself."[29] Dobson adds (sounding somewhat Sacro-Theistical), "The beauty of implementing the principles given to us in Scripture is that they were provided by the Creator of families, and they work in all situations."[30]

3.2.1 Sacro-Clericalism Presence in Congregational Surveys

The survey data also suggests that even though Sacro-Egoism has a strong presence in the McMinnville religious and spiritual community, it is not alone. Many responses of the survey participants were Sacro-Clerical in their expressions of religiosity. This is evident in questions regarding attendance, participation (both personal and familial), authority, priorities, personal spirituality, and the social duties of the church.

Based on the survey results, the Sacro-Clericalists are those who have a high church attendance rate and who do not just show up, but also participate in church-sponsored activities (but do not necessarily participate in extra-church activities besides reading the Bible—a church-sanctioned tome). They themselves are involved and they bring up their children, too, to be involved in the church (46 percent) and to be spiritual (28 percent).

Additionally, they give the church and Scripture the highest authority in their lives (11.6 percent), they relate mainly to the Trinity (10 percent), and they believe that God is beyond them

---

28. Fotana, *Psychology, Religion, and Spirituality*, 90–91.

29. Zohar and Marshall, *Spiritual Intelligence*, 235.

30. Dobson, "Dobson's New Dare," 70.

(11.3 percent). They also feel an obligation to fulfill their duties (50 percent), and they believe that not attending church (17 percent) or working on Sunday is always wrong (5.6 percent). These people demonstrate an embrace and affirmation of the church as an institution from which they gain comfort, connection, and direction.

As far as one church dominating in Sacro-Clericalism, there is a mixed level of responses within the church community; even so, more of the Saint James Catholic Church respondents selected "the Church" as the highest authority in their lives (.07 percent). In fact, beside the McMinnville Covenant Church Youth Group, they were the only ones to mark the church as an authority. Additionally, they (and the First Presbyterian Church) also had the fewest number selecting their "own reason and judgment" as the highest authority in their lives than any other church (.02 percent). They also had the highest percentage of respondents attending church once or more times per week (95.1 percent). Finally, across the board, the Catholic Church had more respondents indicating that it was proper for leaders of religion to speak out on social and moral issues. Based on these responses, a case can be made for Saint James Catholic Church being representative of Sacro-Clericalism.

3.2.2 Sacro-Communalism Presence
in Congregational Surveys

The survey data also showed a Sacro-Communal expression of religiosity in the participants' lives. This is evident in their involvement in activities inside and outside the church (including their involvement in groups from the holistic milieu), their spiritual prioritization, their view of humanity and responses to it.

Many of the participants indicated they were involved in social activities within (68 percent) and outside of the church (20 percent). Bible studies and prayer groups were the most common activities performed within the church; outside of the church, some people indicated that they had attended at least one time Buddhist groups, CancerCare groups, Inter-Faith groups, Taize singing groups, and Women's Spirituality groups.

Concerning their spiritual prioritization, 39.4 percent of participants believed serving God and loving their fellow human beings was "Most important." They also have a strong sense of compassion toward people as 56.7 percent of respondents indicated they thought, "We are sinners needing forgiveness." 46 percent of participants further said, "You should think of others before yourself," 28 percent thought that "Humans are basically good," and 23.3 percent indicated they thought, "All good people will be saved." These people feel a close, sympathetic connection to the community of humanity and take a therapeutic, rather than condemning, approach to their faith.

Based on survey responses regarding group involvement outside of church, the church surveys indicated that the highest percentage of participants involved in extra-church activities/ groups came from the First Presbyterian Church (40 percent). This is potentially indicative of a Sacro-Communal approach to religion, as these activities rest outside of church regulation, yet are not solitary events. Interestingly, the most Sacro-Communal group in McMinnville, based on the survey data, included the participants from the holistic milieu study, which is explained more fully in chapter 4.

3.2.3 Sacro-Theism Presence in Congregational Surveys

A smaller segment of the McMinnville Project can be considered "Sacro-Theist" based on the data survey. Sacro-Theists follow "a religious tendency and desire of the human soul towards an intimate union with the Divinity, or a system growing out of such a tendency and desire."[31] Giving full authority and receiving personal direction from God for their lives, they may be attending church, they may be in the holistic milieu, or they may be doing nothing overtly spiritual outside of their homes (or heads). The Sacro-Theists can be glimpsed in their understanding of authority,

---

31. "Mysticism;" online: http://www.newadvent.org/cathen/10663b.htm.

the cultivation of their relationship with God and/or Jesus, and the manifestation of this relationship.

Even though it may relate more to Sacro-Egoism, clearly a percentage of people who claim that "God" is the highest authority in their life experience this in a direct way unrelated to the church or any community. They feel the presence of God directly speaking to them in their prayers or audibly from above (73.3 percent), giving them direction and purpose in life. They believe that "Spirituality is obeying God's will" (56 percent). They relate most to God, the Father (28 percent), and connect with him both potentially within (56 percent) and beyond them (11.3 percent). They would hold that faith is "believing what we know to be the truth" (22 percent) because God is delivering that truth to human hearts and minds.

Due to the mystical approach and personal realities of Sacro-Theism, it is difficult to completely quantify this approach to religiosity because often its manifestations are unverifiable or indefinable even to the mystic. As Golding suggests, "To provide a more definitive rationale, one must consider a particular vision of religious theism, in connection with a particular person in a particular set of circumstances."[32] The individual nature of Sacro-Theism means that what might lead one person to connect with God outside of the church may not be true for another Sacro-Theist who connects with God within the church. In fact, there are many churches that uphold the notion of new or personal revelation from God (the Mormon Church, the Seventh Day Adventists, the Quakers, etc.).

The First Presbyterian Church surveys also indicated the strongest presence of Sacro-Theism with the greatest percentage of respondents indicating that, in the past, God had 'directly/mystically communicated' with them (31 percent). Furthermore, this church also had the second highest number of respondents who indicated that God was the highest authority in their lives (82.8 percent). Thus, it could be argued that the First Presbyterian Church demonstrated Sacro-Theism more than other churches in

---

32. Golding, *Rationality and Religious Theism*, 27.

the Congregational Study, but, as mentioned earlier, the primary pattern observed suggests that Sacro-Egoism is dominant in the case study churches. Although the structure of this congregational survey may not be too enlightening considering this aspect, future investigations considering the Sacro-Theists could and should be attempted with more specificity.

3.3 Conclusion

Foundationally, when it comes to belief, everyone eventually makes the important choice of what his or her source of authority will be. One cannot be forced to believe something—that is a mental function outside of anyone's control—but one can volitionally give up control to an outside source for a variety of reasons, some beneficial and some oppressive.

The surveys and interviews show that many people choose the Sacro-Egoist route; some choose the Sacro-Communal path; some choose to stay under the Sacro-Clerical path. Once the initial authority is established, then choices are made when it comes to one's path of religion and spirituality. However, this placement of authority can also be removed and placed anew somewhere else many times in a person's life.

Fifty years ago, the McMinnville church scene was much different than today. Church was an accepted part of the general community and frequently a matter of positive focus. An examination of a McMinnville daily newspaper from February of 1970[33] shows multiple articles concerning church services, prayer groups, religious conferences, and church-sponsored sports teams (softball). There was even a short homily presented in its "the Church and World of Today" section.[34] A "Directory of Local Churches" was provided with only traditional Catholic and Protestant denominations listed.[35]

33. "The Church and World of Today," *The News-Register* 104.

34. Henry, "Noah's Son—A Parable," 7.

35. *The News-Register* 104, 7.

A supplemental examination of a newspaper edition from February of 1985 showed less general articles concerning church life distributed within the newspaper. There was just one article about a men's chorus performing at a local church. It also provided information on church services, conferences, and Christian speakers in its "Church news round-up" section. There also was a "Directory of Churches" sections; however, it included some non-traditional spiritual groups such as the Bahá'í Faith group, the First Church of Christ (Scientist), but not the Mormon Church (LDS).[36] The emphasis of the church was definitely not as prevalent as in 1970, but there still was a general conservative presentation of church life.

In modern times, this has changed. The "Religion" section from a newspaper edition from July 7, 2007 provides listings and informational summaries for a variety of churches and spiritual groups, both traditional and from the holistic milieu.[37] This section begins with an announcement concerning the Bahá'í community and ends with a clip about a silent meditation meeting with the New Thought Fellowship. The majority of the informational blurbs still relate to the mainstream groups in McMinnville, but there is a definite change in the presentation in the newspaper. People have more choices now both in and outside of church than every before. As the United Methodist Church pastor put it, "Once the authority regarding religious conviction devolves to the individual, he or she has no choice but to exercise it."[38] The latest newspaper editions in McMinnville tell us that many people are doing just that when it comes to their religiosity.

36. *The News-Register* 119, A4.

37. "Religion," *The News-Register* 142, no. 81.

38. Steve, United Methodist Church pastor, email message to author (June 9, 2007).

4

The Holistic Milieu in the West

4.0 Introduction

THIS CHAPTER PRESENTS RELEVANT data from the McMinnville Project regarding the holistic milieu and provides four key implications from that data concerning the direction the holistic milieu is going in McMinnville—that people in the holistic milieu express their faith more as radical individualists than communally or institutionally, that despite being anti-institutional, they are not necessarily opposed to the notion of Jesus or the use of the Bible, that they are personally committed to their spiritual quests, and that they appreciate and utilize non-traditional avenues of religion and spirituality in their lives. Fox writes, "Renewal implies a new beginning, a new spirit, a new energy unleashed, a new paradigm, a new way to see the world. Enter the phrase 'New Age.'"[1]

It argues that, contrary to Heelas *et al.'s* prediction that "Those forms of spirituality in the West that help people to live in accordance with the deepest, sacred dimension of their own unique lives can be expected to be growing,"[2] the holistic milieu is not usurping the traditional religious domain in people's lives and priorities. It still has a limited presence, but it is not a strong one nor one that will be taking over the spiritual scene very soon, if

1. Fox, "Spirituality for a New Era," 201.
2. Heelas et al., *The Spiritual Revolution*, 7.

at all (based on the statistical data of participation, longevity, etc.). Compared to traditional avenues of spirituality, the holistic milieu is difficult to find, although once found, it is not hard to join.

One of the more difficult aspects of the McMinnville Project's sociological study of religion has involved the defining, locating, and sampling of the alternative spirituality practices. Ellway suggests that, based on religious studies such as Knoblauch's, "Europe displays declining religiosity, but shows how this is qualified by a real takeup of what he [Knoblauch] calls alternative religion, a wider term than 'New Age' which means privatized non-traditional and non-institutional religions."[3]

Concerning spirituality in the United States, Kimball remarks,

> In our increasingly post-Christian culture, the influences and values shaping emerging generations are no longer aligned with Christianity. Emerging generations don't have a basic understanding of the story of the Bible, and they don't have one God as the predominant God to worship. Rather, they are open to all types of faiths, including new mixtures of religions.[4]

Heelas *et al.* mention that these activities and groups are "less obvious" and that they are synonymous with the New Age movement.[5] Heelas states,

> One's initial impression is of an eclectic hotch-potch of beliefs, practices and ways of life. Esoteric or mystical Buddhism, Christianity, Hinduism, Islam and Toaism enter the picture. So do elements from 'pagan' teachings including Celtic, Druidic, Mayan and Native American Indians. An exceedingly wide range of practices—Zen meditations, Wiccan rituals, enlightenment intensive seminars, management trainings, shamanic activities,

---

3. Ellway, "Shopping for Faith or Dropping Your Faith?," 19; online: http://www.csa.com/discoveryguides/religion/overview.php.

4. Kimball, *They Like Jesus But Not the Church*, 16.

5. Heelas et al., *The Spiritual Revolution*, 8.

wilderness events, spiritual therapies, forms of positive thinking—fall under the rubric.[6]

Because of the aforementioned, the holistic milieu, or New Age Movement, has been described as a "cultural fog bank,"[7] "undeniably nebulous"[8] and "subjective-life spirituality"[9]—labels that describe the sometimes-ambiguous, very personal nature of the holistic milieu. Furthermore, Heelas *et al.* refer to the holistic milieu as, " . . . forms of sacred activity which are often grouped together under collective terms like 'body, mind, and spirit', 'New Age', 'alternative' or 'holistic spirituality', and which include (spiritual) yoga, Reiki, meditation, tai chi, aromatherapy, much paganism, rebirthing, reflexology, much Wicca and many more."[10]

Certainly connected to its ubiquitous floating presence is the challenge to find such centers and gathering places of its adherents. Obviously, there is no "Church of the Holistic Milieu" officially set up in McMinnville; rather, there are pockets of people coming together to share a commonality of faith/spirituality different from the mainstream understanding. Not only are these assemblies difficult to find, but they are also difficult to scientifically examine. Very often, people from the outside are welcomed in as seekers, but not always as observers (from personal experience during the McMinnville Project).

Despite these difficulties, the holistic milieu in McMinnville was researched as thoroughly as possible. What follows is an analysis of participants' understandings of religion, spirituality, and the role of the individual in McMinnville society.

This chapter presents the findings to suggest that Sacro-Egoism is not just a congregational domain phenomenon; it is also present in the holistic milieu data. Most holistic milieu participants demonstrated a Sacro-Egoist approach in their survey responses

6. Heelas, *The New Age Movement*, 1.

7. Bainbridge, *The Sociology of Social Movements*, 390.

8. Partridge, "Truth, Authority, and Epistemological Individualism in New Age Thought," 78.

9. Heelas et al., *The Spiritual Revolution*, 5.

10. Ibid., 7.

when interviewed. Four areas connecting the holistic milieu are discussed—individualism, sources of authority, personal commitment to spirituality, and tolerance toward non-traditional avenues of spirituality and religiosity. It also examines the role and priority of Jesus and the Bible in the lives of the holistic milieu survey participants.

Next, the unique characteristics of the holistic milieu, the ones that set it apart from the congregational studies, are explored. This section also addresses the issues of Rational Choice Theory, the presence of Sacro-Communalism in the holistic milieu, and the holistic milieu participants' cautionary disposition. The chapter ends with concluding comments on the future of the holistic milieu in McMinnville.

4.1 Holistic Milieu Presence in McMinnville

After an extensive search, several holistic milieu groups were identified, (the Bahá'ís, the MAC Contemplative group, Seven Thunders Zen/Christian Group, and The New Thought Ministry) although others may exist underground, unverifiable or observable except through personal, private (human) revelation. Some of these groups have been around for a decade; others are new to the area in the past few years. As Hammett remarks, "There are many who are spiritually minded and many who are serious about their spiritual journey who cannot find their place in most of the existing institutional churches."[11] Their long-standing presence (or absence) in the McMinnville community will be addressed first, followed by description and attendance information for the holistic milieu groups that were discovered.

4.1.1 Longitudinal Holistic Milieu Activity

As with the Kendal Project, phone directories from three different years were selected for examination of religious offerings—1970,

11. Hammett, *Spiritual Leadership in a Secular Age*, 5.

1985, and 2007. Under "CHURCH" in the *McMinnville & Amity Yellow Pages* directory from 1970, nineteen different religious groups' phone number listings were provided;[12] of those, the only listings that could possibly be considered unorthodox or outside of traditional avenues of Christianity were the Christian Science Church, the Jehovah's Witnesses Kingdom Hall, and the Mormon Church. No other holistic milieu centers (such as the Bahá'ís, MAC Contemplative Group, Buddhists, etc.) were provided, although listings were provided for four Chiropractic Physicians and one Naturopathic Physician.

Under "Yamhill County Churches" in the *PhoneBook: Residential Edition For Yamhill County, 1985,* twenty-one religious groups' phone listings were provided.[13] As with the directory from 1970,[14] no holistic milieu centers were listed except for the Bahá'í Faith Center. Under "Organizations & Service Clubs," a few non-traditional groups listings were provided such as the International Order of the Odd Fellows, and the Masonic Lodge, but no holistic milieu groups.[15] Under "Chiropractic Physicians," six listings were provided.[16]

In 2007, the situation had changed somewhat, but the names of the holistic milieu groups were still as scarce to find as in the previous years' books. There was no listing for "Alternative Spirituality," "New Age," "Spiritual," or even "Religion." There was one listing under "Holistic Practitioners" for a LPC.[17] There were four listings under "Naturopathic Doctors ND," but the one advertisement was focused on health issues and not spiritual well being.

There were thirty-nine churches listed in the 2007 directory, but all were either traditional or non-denominational.[18] No holistic milieu centers were listed at all. The only holistic milieu listing

12. "McMinnville & Amity Yellow Pages," 18–19.
13. *PhoneBook: Residential Edition For Yamhill County,* 122–123.
14. Ibid., 19.
15. Ibid., 149–152.
16. Ibid., 121–122.
17. *YellowBook (2007–2008): Greater Yamhill County,* 275.
18. Ibid., 146–148.

found in the residential section of the phonebook was for the Baháʼí Center; neither the listings for the McMinnville Contemplative Center, the Seven Thunders, nor the New Thought Ministry were found. This is more evidence that finding the holistic milieu in McMinnville was facilitated greatly by Neil who connected me with the right people. Without his assistance, tracking down the four groups would have been even harder than it was.

4.2 The Holistic Milieu Presence Within the Congregational Domain

From these characteristics of Sacro-Egoism and the statistical data compiled in both the congregational surveys and the Street Survey, it is evident that the habit of many McMinnvillians is to uphold their personal authority over the local institutions. Killen suggests, "Religious commitment here continues to be fluid, individualistic, egalitarian in structure, focused on results, and episodic."[19] Thus, authority has shifted from the church to the individual. Furseth and Repstad state, "Traditional authority is based on habit and the absence of reflection upon alternative forms of domination."[20] If this is true, then traditional authority has diminished remarkably, and McMinnvillians are seeking their authority outside of traditional bounds. It is as Hunt suggests: "The individual spiritual quest, where it exists, is inward-looking and tending towards narcissism and egoistic desires rather than being expressed in terms of communities or through institutional settings."[21]

Based on the data compiled in the congregational surveys and the Street Survey, there is no paradigmal shift from traditional church activities to the holistic milieu in McMinnville. A few people in every case study church participated or had tried alternative spirituality practices associated with the New Age Movement, but their statistical significance was negligible considering the size of

---

19. Killen, "Religious Futures in the None Zone," 183.

20. Furseth and Repstad, *An Introduction to the Sociology of Religion*, 145.

21. Hunt, *Religion and Everyday Life*, 69.

the church-going population and the population of McMinnville in general—regular holistic milieu attendees amounted to less than ¼ of 1 percent of the entire population in McMinnville. Furthermore, there is the possibility that, like some Christians, people active within the holistic milieu might even be inflating their own attendance numbers for similar reasons.[22]

As Furseth and Repstad suggest, "In a Western context, a growing support for alternative religiosity or relatively new minority religions such as Islam, Hinduism, or Buddhism, may lead a scholar to exaggerate the support for these traditions and overlook the fact that the large majority still supports the Christian tradition."[23] However, even if the practitioners (or some scholars) are not guilty of enhancing their attendance records, the involvement numbers are still low.

Yet, despite their lack of participation in holistic milieu activities, the survey participants still displayed a high degree of tolerance for alternative or complementary non-church forms of spirituality (See Figure 10). Roof remarks, "Eclectic styles of religion and spirituality flourish within the region. Partly, this is because of the openness toward diversity and the fact that people within religious communities feel free to absorb aspects of other traditions in their spiritual lives."[24] Some 48.7 percent indicated that they thought alternative forms of spirituality could be useful for some Christians; 15.3 percent indicated that they thought alternative forms of spirituality are helpful for Christians. Some 10.7 percent of respondents thought that alternative forms of spirituality "have things to teach Christianity." This is compared to the 18.7 percent of survey respondents who said alternative forms of spirituality are unacceptable for Christians and the 23.3 percent who said alternative forms of spirituality are unnecessary for Christians.

22. Hadaway and Marler, "How Many Americans Attend Worship Each Week? An Alternative Approach to Measurement," 308.

23. Furseth and Repstad, *An Introduction to the Sociology of Religion*, 126.

24. Roof, *Religion & Public Life in the Pacific Region*, 175.

	Unacceptable	Unnecessary	Useful	Helpful	Things To Teach
Non-Church Forms:	18.7%	23.3%	48.7%	15.3%	10.7%

Figure 10 - Tolerance of Alternative Spirituality Activities: Congregational Survey Results

Also, when asked if they believe that it is proper and beneficial for church leaders to speak on a variety of social topics, the majority (75.5 percent) said it was proper. Disconnected from their other answers, this could suggest a strong expression of Sacro-Clericalism; however, more likely, the participants are tolerant of the pastors speaking about controversial matters so that they can receive more information on the topic to make up their minds later. "Speaking Out" on social matters is not the same thing as condemning the people doing them.

Nevertheless, overall, the respondents were more tolerant than condemning when it came to their judgment on holistic milieu practices. They are more tolerant of the freedom of any person to investigate other spiritual avenues; however, they are not actively or personally pursuing these alternative spirituality groups or paths in substantial numbers.

4.3 Holistic Milieu McMinnville Demographics

With such a small sampling, it is difficult to get a full grasp of the demographics of this group, but the holistic milieu surveys do provide some information (See Figure 11). In the holistic milieu survey, 60 percent of respondents indicated they were female, 20 percent indicated they were male, and 20 percent chose to not respond). Regarding their age, 60 percent of respondents indicated that they were age fifty to sixty-four, 10 percent indicated that they were age thirty-five to thirty-nine, and 10 percent indicated that they were age sixty-five to sixty-nine. Concerning their home life,

70 percent indicated they were married and 10 percent indicated that they were living alone with children. Furthermore, 30 percent marked that they owned their homes without a mortgage, 30 percent marked that they had homes with mortgages, and 30 percent marked that they were renting.

When queried about their educational backgrounds, 80 percent indicated that they were attending or had attended a college. Also, 20 percent indicated that they were in full-time education—10 percent marked that they were in graduate school. Some 20 percent were studying arts and humanities, 10 percent were studying business or economics, 10 percent were studying engineering, 10 percent were studying biology, 10 percent were studying the natural sciences, 20 percent were studying medicine, and 10 percent were studying religion.

	Percent
Female	60
Male	40
Attended College	80
Married	70
Single	20
Divorced/Separated	10
Full-Time Work	10
Republican	10
Democrat	50

Figure 11 - General Demographic makeup:
Holistic Milieu Survey Results

When asked about their vocations, 30 percent of the holistic milieu participants indicated they were in part-time work, 10 percent indicated that they were in full-time work, 20 percent indicated that they were retired, and 10 percent indicated that they were looking after the home. Furthermore, 20 percent indicated that they were employed in a professional or technical occupation,

20 percent indicated that they were a manger or a senior admin-
istrator, and 20 percent indicated "other" when asked about their
occupation.

Thus, one could generalize that a participant in the holistic milieu is most likely to be a married female, attending either
undergraduate or graduate college, employed part-time, and a
politically liberal. However, the small number of holistic milieu
participants involved in this study makes it difficult to fully ascertain. As with the Kendal Project, questions regarding income and
ethnicity were left off, which would have added to the investigation of this demographic group.

4.4 Sacro-Egoism in the Holistic Milieu

The Sacro-Egoism factor was frequently seen, heard, and observed
from the holistic milieu participants in McMinnville in the surveys and interviews. It manifests itself much in the same ways as
the congregational surveys showed, but with some key differences.
The aspects the holistic milieu shares with the congregational
domain include 1) a radical individualism 2) a disdain for traditional authority 3) a personal commitment to spirituality and 4)
an openness and toleration for non-traditionalist avenues of spirituality. Sacro-Egoism in the holistic milieu differs concerning its
prioritization of Jesus and the Bible.

Sacro-Egoism in the holistic milieu begins with the individual seeking spiritual connections from alternative expressions of
faith. This makes sense because as Hunt notes, "Individualism is at
the heart of the network of ideas and the identification of New Age
Spirituality."[25] Flanagan and Jupp add, "In the quest for health of
body and soul, the holistic opportunities presented by spirituality
are available for the self to appropriate and to find its own criteria
of validation within. Holistic spirituality offers the self the prospect of ultimate self-mastery."[26]

25. Hunt, *Religion and Everyday Life*, 153.
26. Flanagan and Jupp, *A Sociology of Spirituality*, 6.

4.4.1 Radical Individualism

People in the McMinnville holistic milieu hold their own personal understanding of religion/God/spirituality above traditional religion and even their own personal culture and environment. According to Partridge, this is due to the fact that "For New Age epistemology, the self becomes supremely significant: not only is the self able to discover truth, but the truth it seeks is within the self."[27] In a very real sense, the self is understood to be ultimate source for spirituality and religious direction.

This notion is evident when one holistic milieu interviewee stated about church life in general, "The individual comes in by themselves and leaves by themselves. You are responsible for your life to take control and to direct your life to the highest potential."

The Chair of the board of directors from the New Thought Ministry stated,

> Our "new thoughts" enter the Universal Mind of God, are transformed and mirrored back into new experiences in our lives. New Thought teaches how to connect directly with the Creator, that we each have the inner power to change our lives as we desire (through the various laws of the universe as proven by quantum physics). We have a direct path to God through the raising of our consciousness. We teach ultimate Truth within our God-centered Consciousness (not someplace outside of us). We are the direct link to God.[28]

The starting point for this group and others like it is the individual, which cumulates into a group. In this respect, many people within the holist milieu are Sacro-Egoist or Sacro-Communal.

Every holistic milieu survey demonstrated this mind-set in some form or fashion. They were involved in alternative spirituality practices because 1) they were disappointed in what organized religion offered to them; 2) they felt that they, themselves,

27. Partridge, "Truth, Authority and Epistemological Individualism in New Age Thought," 78.

28. Joanne, Chair, Board of Directors, New Age Ministries, email message to author (June 26, 2007).

should be the ones deciding what was right for them, spiritually; and 3) they wished to belong to a community outside of traditional boundaries. As Wuthnow states, "Metaphysical teachings, of course, encourage an expansive self and collective hope."[29] Their connection with God, the Supreme Force, the spiritual life was about their individual understanding in the community and nothing about what any formal institution instructed them to do or think.

4.4.2 Sources of Authority

In many ways, according to Heelas *et al.*, individualism is the starting place for many involved in the holistic milieu who are disenchanted with the traditional experience of spirituality that appeals to a higher, earthly authority or who were " . . . imposing pre-packaged life-as values, beliefs or injunctions."[30]

Another common trait for those involved in the holistic milieu was a definite (and at times paradoxical as they continued to participate in traditional churches) dislike or disregard for organized religion. In this matter, Partridge claims, "Only personal experience, it is argued, can provide immediate and uncontaminated access to truth, particularly truth in the sphere of the spiritual/ transpersonal. Mediated truth, communicated by sacred texts, by the Church, by society cannot be trusted."[31] Grace Davie adds strength to this notion when she says, "What I have said, and reaffirm here, is that belief that detaches itself from institutional commitment begins to drift away from the orthodoxies endorsed by the institution in question."[32] Aldridge states, "Organized religion

29. Wuthnow, *Spiritual Marketplace*, 208.

30. Heelas et al., *The Spiritual Revolution*, 30.

31. Partridge, "Truth, Authority, and Epistemological Individualism in New Age Thought," 85.

32. Davie, "Praying Alone? Church-going in Britain and Social Capital: A Reply to Steve Bruce," 333.

as conventionally understood in the Judaeo-Christian tradition is rejected as authoritarian and spiritually arid."[33]

Attesting to this, in his interview, Neil stated of his Methodist past, "Some of the Bible stories . . . were kind of interesting and I paid attention to them, but they were more like stories around the camp-fire, folk-stories." For him, the Bible was an interesting work of fiction, but was not a window into heaven. He sought for years to make a connection to the Divine without much success.

In her interview, too, Laura explained her disenchantment with mainstream religion and her approval of the holistic milieu. She stated, "The breadth and depth of material attracts me to alternative spirituality groups; mainstream religion seems dead to me. It has a superficial approach to relating to God and spirituality. It can be limiting in understanding of the direct experience of being."

In fact, a personal experience with marijuana was the first way Neil "turned onto" spirituality in a way that he had never experienced before. As Neil put it, "The spiritual world was very provocative to me like never before experienced in the Church." Based on Hunt's assertion, this could be considered " . . . an ecstatic and magical form of activity and an opportunity for the individual to indulge in the irrational against the enforced rationality of formal and bureaucratically structured organizations and issues."[34] Smoking marijuana is a crime in most parts of the United States (although it became legal to purchase recreational marijuana in Colorado and Washington in 2012 and Alaska and Oregon in 2015); moreover, it has been generally considered taboo in traditional church thought.

Neil broke with all authorities to find his connection with God through the use of psychedelics. Partridge notes, "Psychedelics enable people to breach the fence between their conditioned minds and the larger spiritual environment."[35] For both Neil and Laura, the holistic milieu provides spiritual direction, nourishment, and vitality that the traditional church does not offer to them. Olds

---

33. Aldridge, *Religion in the Contemporary World*, 209.

34. Hunt, *Religion and Everyday Life*, 151.

35. Partridge, *The Re-Enchantment of the West: Volume 2*, 91.

states, "The New Age affirms the primacy of personal choice and responsibility a uniquely human and deeper than gender, status, security, or external authority."[36]

Yet, there are people that are not part of any traditional avenues of spirituality who do not consider themselves part of the holistic milieu. They have taken their radical individualism that much further still. One survey participant, Rick, said,

> I'll attempt to answer the questions best I can but these questions don't quite 'hit the spot' for me . . . my interest & daily practice is Zazen, especially Soto-Zen.[37] Terms such as spirituality, religious & God, aren't really considerations. My practice is not about achieving some special state of mind or preparing for an afterlife. It's living and accepting life, each & every moment just as it is.[38]

The holistic milieu surveys, in particular, suggest that church, as an institutional resource of help, was of low importance to the participants. When asked, "Which of the following most closely describes your attitude to mainstream Christianity? Are you . . . (Please Circle One)," 62.5 percent of survey respondents said they were not committed Christians or were indifferent to Christianity. Several people mentioned they still supported Christian values (37.5 percent), but they were not attending church regularly. It is hard to tell exactly when these people stopped going to church because only three people said they stopped from ages 16-30. The rest of the participants left that question blank.

4.4.3 The Holistic Milieu Understanding of Jesus

Part of the holistic milieu or New Age movement is a change in the way Jesus is embraced and viewed. He is still greatly admired and

36. Olds, "The New Age: Historical and Metaphysical Foundations," 69.

37. Zazen is Zen meditation, usually performed in the lot position; Soto-Zen is undirected meditation wherein one attempts to detach from the mind's usual ideas and identities to return later to fully engage in the present moment.

38. Rick, holistic milieu participant, email message to author (June 22, 2007).

a model for many in the holistic milieu; however, as Lynch suggests, "The divine is no longer placed in a realm above and beyond the natural world, nor located simply in the person of Jesus, but is spread throughout the emerging cosmos."[39] The story of Jesus is a lesson that all can potentially become divine, either within the holistic milieu or in other channels of faith—both traditional and alternative.

This high but untraditional estimation of Jesus by the holistic milieu survey participants is seen in their responses. Some 77.8 percent indicated that they thought, "Jesus was the son of God;" however, 33.3 percent also said, "Jesus was just a man." This does not necessarily negate his divinity or elevate him to top spiritual status. As Lynch states, "Jesus thus becomes divine through his participation in the one divine spirit rather than being a distinctive divine figure in his own right."[40]

In fact, one holistic milieu survey participant wrote on her survey, "Jesus was God incarnate—fully human/divine but he was not the only divine character or personification of God—Jesus is but one face of the person of God." Another indicated that although she thought Jesus was God, she wrote in, "As we all are." To these holistic milieu participants, Jesus has the important role of being one of many people who have reached spiritual perfection.

4.4.4 The Holistic Milieu Understanding of The Bible

Interestingly, a high percentage of the holistic milieu survey participants indicated that they were significantly connected to Christianity and were not condemning of the Bible. Some 33.3 percent of respondents indicated that they considered themselves, "committed, church going Christians," 22.2 percent said that they were "Not committed Christian, but support Christian values," and only 22 percent said that they were "indifferent to Christianity."

---

39. Lynch, *The New Spirituality*, 37.
40. Ibid., 44.

One survey participant wrote in his survey, "I think the Bible has been dabbled with, but I think it holds up pretty good. I think what Jesus is purported to have said, he probably did say because it is so inherently true. There are other holy scriptures, though, besides the Bible."

4.4.5 Personal Commitment to Spirituality

It is evident from the holistic milieu survey data and in the interviews that its participants placed a high value on their spirituality. One interviewee indicated that he thought there was "no separation" between the alternative therapies and spirituality. This makes sense because as Heelas *et al.* state, "Virtually all practitioners and a great many of their participants are holistically orientated, attaching importance to subjective-life spirituality, with life-as religion scarcely in evidence."[41]

Thus, 77.8 percent of respondents indicated that they were a "Spiritual Person." Furthermore, when asked to rank the importance of spirituality in their lives, 88.9 percent gave it a "10." Only 11.1 percent elected not to answer the question. When discussing why they took up a holistic milieu activity, 66.7 percent said that they were "looking for spiritual growth."

The surveys were not the only place where an indication of a personal commitment to spirituality could be seen. Unsolicited comments offered good insight into the commitment level of the participants, too. These comments were generally of three types: ones that more greatly defined the survey-takers understanding of God/spirituality, ones that clarified the survey-takers personal journeys, and personal salutations and wishes for me. Concerning their spirituality, one holistic milieu participant wrote, "Spirituality is a relationship to God." Another provided, "Reality has a spiritual dimension." So, spirituality has a relational quality that revolves around the reality of the individual.

41. Heelas et al., *The Spiritual Revolution*, 30.

One section, in particular, led to significant comments. Question 29 of the holistic milieu survey asked, "What would you say are the three most important problems facing you, personally, these days (Please write in)?" Comments that were given included, "Write intellectual papers for Masters Degree," "Losing weight," "My Dad is near death," "My daughter hasn't spoken to me for a year," "My troubled marriage," "Health and vitality," "Family harmony," and "Financial stability."

There was an obvious lack of spiritual prioritization expressed in these comments, although there was a definite relational and personal health focus. As Hunt puts it, "Not only is the New Age rampantly individualistic in many respects, it is also highly secular in some of its trajectories, and marks an essentially inward-looking endeavour."[42]

4.4.6 Openness and Toleration of Non-traditional Beliefs

Part of the holistic milieu is an embrace of alternative expressions of spirituality from those in the gathering. Kimball remarks of those outside of the church, "They are aware of global faiths and most place a strong value on the belief that everyone should believe what they want to and that no single religion should claim exclusivity over others."[43] These people are able to come together in these groups with their unique approaches to spirituality without the fear of condemnation or retribution.

One of the more extreme unsolicited statements from a member of the holistic milieu was that the participant had a "close encounter with Bigfoot, which included clear telepathy. Also, [I had] an angel encounter." In the holistic milieu group with which the aforementioned interviewee was involved, "Participants are not called upon to be anything other than what they are at heart."[44]

42. Hunt, *Religion and Everyday Life*, 155-156.

43. Kimball, *They Like Jesus But Not the Church*, 168–169.

44. Heelas et al., *The Spiritual Revolution*, 30.

Furthermore, "They [holistic milieu activities] can be practiced without coming into conflict with everyday occupational roles and secular demands."[45] The holistic milieu participants find this comforting and a secure place to exercise their spirituality.

That being said, both holistic milieu interviewees currently were also attending local churches. Neil mentioned, "I have a personal theology that embraces most, pretty much, fairly tight-bound level of orthodoxy. In fact, my wife and I are in the process of joining a very conservative church."

Laura, too, was attending a church. She said, "Now I go to church as a person available to be to service to others. I do not have personal needs as a seeker there anymore; I am there to be of support." One holistic milieu survey participant indicated concerning their attitude toward mainstream Christianity that she was "Mostly Christian but non-exclusive."

The holistic milieu participants in McMinnville had not completely abandoned traditional avenues of Christianity despite their criticism of it.

4.5 The Holistic Milieu Characteristics

There are a few specific traits that seem specific to the holistic milieu. These include a belief in and involvement with alternative spirituality practices that holistic milieu participants consider spiritual in nature, a plurality or dualism in religious activity that allows for dual membership in traditional and alternative practices, a strong sense of community, and a cautionary outlook in life and relationships.

4.5.1 Belief in the Spirituality of Holistic Activities

First and foremost, the holistic milieu participants experienced or were clearly aware of a spiritual connection in the alternative spirituality activities they were involved in outside of church.

45. Hunt, *Religion and Everyday Life*, 151.

Some 90 percent of participants indicated that they had recently and regularly participated in a spiritual activity that they considered spiritual or religious in nature. Furthermore, holistic milieu participants were involved with the holistic milieu activities for an extended period of time. This involvement was not a one-time affair but continuous in their lives. Their involvement in the holistic milieu also was more diffused than in the congregational study; 90 percent of holistic milieu participants had tried multiple alternative activities.

4.5.2 Rational Choice Theory in the Holistic Milieu

One of the distinct holistic milieu characteristics revolved around their involvement in both traditional and alternative spirituality activities at the same time. From the survey data and their interviews, it is evident that they were operating with a sense of pluralism that is common to holistic milieu participants. Some 30 percent of McMinnville holistic milieu participants indicated they were going to church and another 40 percent said they were supportive of Christianity even though they did not attend church regularly. As Partridge puts it, "Its [New Age] eclectic pluralism simply undermines any attempt to discern a single concept of truth or authority without being procrustean in certain respects."[46] Aldridge adds, "New Age groups are strikingly pluralistic. There is no problem in participating in a variety of groups and practices to suit the individual's needs."[47]

Both Neil and Laura show very strong signs of a pluralistic, tolerant understanding of church life that allows for them to be both part of the holistic milieu and part of the traditional church life at the same time. Yet, there was not necessarily an acceptance of the conservative church route with which they were supplementing their faith; in some ways, it seems akin to Rational Choice Theory, in that they were using the traditional avenues to

46. Partridge, "Truth, Authority, and Epistemological Individualism in New Age Thought," 77.

47. Aldridge, *Religion in the Contemporary World*, 207.

acquire access to service the community, not because they fully embrace the theology of their churches. As Furseth and Repstad state, "According to Rational Choice Theory, social actors will always seek to obtain their goals with the least amount of risk and cost involved."[48] Thus, a person's involvement depends upon their goals, comfort threshold, and spiritual valuing.

Both Neil and Laura fit well within the spectrum of holistic milieu participants according to Heelas.[49] He states, " . . . the 'fully engaged' are those who have given over their lives to the spiritual quest; 'serious part-timers' whose spirituality is compartmentalized as part of their life (albeit a serious part); 'casual part-timers' are basically consumers interested in exotic/esoteric things, but are wary of getting deeply involved."

Based on their surveys and interviews, it could be speculated that Neil was fully engaged and Laura was a serious part-timer, but both were very sincere and serious about their spiritual journeys.

4.5.3 Sacro-Communalism

A seemingly paradoxical characteristic of the holistic milieu participants was a strong sense of community that embraced people with a strong sense of individualism. Stephen Hunt states, "The movement is sufficiently broad, however, to embrace all-comers."[50] The holistic milieu survey responses also provided some light in this matter. In the survey, several people indicate that they joined their particular groups, "to meet like minded people." They were looking for a spiritual support group where they could be fed (by a personal and community experience) and led (through individual and community enlightenment). As one survey participant wrote, "I like the teachings of my community because I like what my spiritual leader says and what he says we are to do. He wants us

48. Furseth and Repstad, *An Introduction to the Sociology of Religion*, 117.
49. Heelas, *The New Age Movement*, 117-119.
50. Hunt, *Religion and Everyday Life*, 159.

to be free in our thinking, he wants us to question, but there are certain laws we have to obey or we will suffer."

Additionally, Both Neil and Laura voiced their appreciation for their approach to spirituality and spoke highly of the benefits it had brought to their lives. In his interview, Neil confided about a family crisis where he was estranged from his wife and children. He said, "There were some overwhelmingly ripping mystical experiences that made that happen. That I was contacted and my wife was contacted by the Central Force in the Universe in a profound, jarring sort of way that brought me back to my family and sort of brought us back together." The holistic milieu had a therapeutic aspect to it that helped heal, not only spiritual wounds, but emotional and physical ones as well. It helped bring Neil back into community with his loved ones.

Laura, too, in her interview, opened up and shared her past experiences of church life. She said, "As a youth, I never felt connected in a way that I felt I should be. Intuitively, I felt there was way that I should be connecting; I thought I must not be very spiritual since I was not. Now I feel connected." Before, she had felt disconnected from God despite being deeply involved in church (her father was a Methodist minister; later, he became a Presbyterian minister instead); however, with her husband and their new-found embrace of the holistic movement, she felt comforted and part of a spiritual community.

4.5.4 Cautionary Disposition

Another provocative aspect of the holistic milieu is its participants' seemingly hyper-cautious response to outside investigation. All-too-frequently, when asked if I could observe a holistic group in action, do a demographic count, and distribute a survey, the contact person would ask, "Why do you want to know that about us?" Despite any further explanations and promises of innocuous intent, they would often reply, "I do not think we would be comfortable discussing our spiritual life with you." Their response went beyond privacy, and I sensed they were threatened by the notion of an academic study of their belief system.

This is not mere paranoia; historically, the New Age Movement and the holistic milieu have been criticized, chastised, and ridiculed by others in mainstream religion.[51] Concerning the traditionalist appraisal of the holistic milieu, Partridge explains, "What they see as New Age immanentism has prompted not only the Catholic Church but also other Christian Churches to attack the movement as a form of modern paganism."[52] They often consider any spiritual approach outside of the orthodox world to be a cult, " . . . the term 'cult' being adopted from Evangelical Christians as the appropriate label for the despised new religions."[53]

Just on the sales website page of Josh McDowell and Bob Hostetler's book, *The New Tolerance: How A Cultural Movement Threatens To Destroy You, Your Faith, And Your Children*, one reads,

> Best-selling author Josh McDowell and Bob Hostetler unmask the true nature of the cultural movement of "tolerance" in this powerful release. It will not only help you to understand it, but equip you to counter its insidious effects on your faith and your children. In addition, the authors teach you how to: neutralize this threat by discerning truth from error, teach your children to discern between acceptance and approval, and lovingly respond to a hostile culture that seems willing to tolerate just about anything except biblical truth.[54]

Evangelicals are not the only Christian group to criticize the holistic milieu. The Catholic Church also has condemned this

51. Larsen, *Straight Answers on the New Age*; Newport, *The New Age Movement and the Biblical Worldview*; Whitemarsh and Bill Reisman, *Subtle Serpent*.

52. Clarke, *New Religions in Global Perspective*, 37.

53. Melton, "The Fate of NRMs and Their Detractors in Twenty-First Century America," 232.

54. Available from http://resources.family.org/product/id/101899.do.

New Age movement. The *Pontifical Councils for Culture and Inter-religious Dialogue* warned Catholics that

> It must unfortunately be admitted that there are too many cases where Catholic centres of spirituality are actively involved in diffusing New Age religiosity in the Church. This would of course have to be corrected, not only to stop the spread of confusion and error, but also so that they might be effective in promoting true Christian spirituality.[55]

Furthermore, Jesuit Catholic Priest Father Mitch Pacwa called the New Age movement, "downright dangerous."[56] It is clear that both Evangelical Christian groups and the Catholic Church are actively fighting against New Age beliefs and considers New Age groups to be generally spiritually harmful to Christianity and the world.

With this in mind, it is no wonder that many in the holistic milieu are reticent to divulge their innermost religious/spiritual beliefs and feelings. In one interview, one person said that she had "learned to live her spiritual life underground" because of the hostility she has experienced from mainline Christians. Another mentioned that she does not let anyone know at the church she is attending that she also embraces New Age spirituality. When I sent a short email to the New Thought group (found on their website), my email went through four people before anyone replied.

I found a great deal of information from their web site, but I asked three supplemental questions: 1) How long has New Thought been in existence in McMinnville?; 2) How many attendees do you normally have during the week (Sundays and during your Silent Meditations)?; and 3) Would you consider yourselves part of the New Age Movement or do you consider yourselves another facet of religion?

55. *Pontifical Councils for Culture and Interreligious Dialogue: Section 6.2.* online: http://www.vatican.va/roman_curia/pontifical_councils/interelg/documents/rc_pc_interelg_doc_20030203_new-age_en.html#6.2.%20Practical%20steps.

56. Pacwa, *Catholics and the New Age*, 191–204.

In the final email, which included the members' exchanges about my request, one person had written, "Seems harmless. You might want to reply to this guy."[57] Apparently, there was some question as to my motivation by the group; perhaps they had others try to trick them into giving up information used later to hurt them somehow.

A cautionary disposition was evident in the responses; it made arranging the interviews and surveys that much more difficult. Being such a small segment of society, it makes sense that they would feel "ganged up on" or self-preservative. Many of the beliefs of the holistic milieu practitioners are still considered taboo in traditional churches. If knowledge about their beliefs made it back to their home churches, they could risk exclusion or embarrassment.

4.6 The Future of the Holistic Milieu in McMinnville (and the West)

Based on their sociological study of religion in Kendal, Heelas *et al.* predict:

> The decline of religious capital [or authority], then, has not resulted in a world of atheists—a world which would make life very difficult for holistic spiritual practitioners. Instead, the development of cultural renderings of holistic themes has no doubt encouraged, and been encouraged by, beliefs of "life-force" or "spiritual" variety, and has generated a "spiritual capital" which will increasingly take over the role once played by having been brought up in the Christian faith.[58]

This prediction is based on the assumption that the trend (called barely observable by many) in Kendal will continue to grow until it overtakes the religious scene once dominated by traditional religion. The problem with this notion is that it assumes

57. New Thought Ministry inter-group, first email message to author (June 25, 2007).

58. Heelas et al., *The Spiritual Revolution*, 134.

much about the morbidity of traditional faith and the flourishing of the holistic milieu.

Referring to the presence of New Age thought that embraces Eastern religion, Bruce claims, "Britons . . . are not worshipping Shiva or Vishnu or Ganesh. They are not following the paths of Buddhist monasticism. They are adopting the most plastic philosophical strands and then adapting them."[59]

According to the McMinnville Project data, what is happening with the holistic milieu in McMinnville at most falls more along the lines of Steve Bruce's conclusion than Heelas and Woodhead's. Yes, there are some people in the traditional congregations engaging in alternative spirituality practices, but they are doing them more out of fashion or curiosity than religious fulfillment (based on their responses that indicate no religious association). There are also a very minor percentage of people in McMinnville active in various New Age movements who are very serious about their spirituality, but their numbers are very small considering the size of the city.

59. Bruce, *God is Dead*, 139.

5

The Unchurched in the West

5.0 Introduction

FEW COULD ARGUE THAT America's religious landscape has changed dramatically in the past fifty years. Presently, it has been estimated that nearly 30 percent of US citizens may be "Unchurched";[1] that is, they are not involved in organized religion. In 2015, the Pew Research Center released a report asserting, "The Christian share of the US population is declining, while the number of US adults who do not identify with any organized religion is growing."[2] Sociologist McCloud asserts, "Many of those who left their religious traditions moved to other ones. Yet some did not. A third trend in contemporary American religion entails the increasing numbers of people who do not affiliate with any religious organization."[3] It is growing easier to encounter people who live religiously outside the traditional fold.

Regarding faith inside of Oregon but within the Pacific Northwest, Roof remarks, "There is considerable freedom for

1. Wetzstein, "Christians on the Retreat in the U.S. as the Number of Unchurched Surge;" online: http://www.washingtontimes.com/news/2015/may/12/americans-less-christian-more-unaffiliated-survey-/?page=all.

2. *Pew Research Center*, May 12, 2015; online: http://www.pewforum.org/2015/05/12/americas-changing-religious-landscape/.

3. McCloud, "Liminal Subjectivities and Religious Change, 297.

people to believe and practice faith, or no faith, in the Pacific region."[4] Thus, the unchurched are an important and influential part of Oregonian society, but in many ways, their religious and spiritual beliefs are unknown. The McMinnville Project Street Survey opened a window into the variegated world of these non-participating citizens in that city and provided clues of overall Pacific Northwest religiosity.[5]

The Unchurched segment of Oregonian society, potentially as large as 80 percent of the population (based on the Baylor Survey of Religion: 2006),[6] is the most ubiquitous group to analyze because it is impossible to narrow down their location. It is not as if one can go to a local eatery, bowling alley, or pub and find scores of people hanging around *as an identifiable group* who are unattached or not associated with churches.

This Unchurched group is generally defined in society as "Those who have not attended a church service in the past six months, other than on holidays such as Easter or Christmas, or events such as a funeral."[7] Hale states, "The Unchurched are not only not involved in the life of the church, but are also less likely than the churched to be involved in any type of organization."[8]

Moreover, based on the findings in *A Summary of Qualitative Research on the Unchurched*, "Most believe that it is not necessary to attend a house of worship in order to be religious. They feel

4. Roof, "Religion in the Pacific Region: Demographic Patterns," 32.

5. On the day of the Street Survey, 30.7 percent elected not to participate at all, 26.0 percent surveyed were not attending a local church. If 19.8 percent of the non-participating people went to church but chose not to take the survey, then, on the day of the Street Survey, twenty-seven people potentially were attending church (41.5 percent) while thirty-eight stayed home (58.4 percent). This is a relatively high figure, but if one considers that in the Survey, 33 percent of the surveyed said that they attended church once or less a month, then the potential number of church attendees on that day potentially could drop 33 percent and the number attending that day would more likely be around twenty-nine, which fits well into Finke and Stark's data for the least-churched state in the U.S.A.

6. Online: http://www.baylor.edu/isreligion/index.php?id=40634.

7. "Ratio of 'Unchurched' Up Sharply Since 1991," 15.

8. Hale, *The Unchurched*, 175.

that one can be just as close to God anywhere—in the woods or at home."[9] According to McCloud, "Religion continues to be important in individuals' everyday lives—even for those who do not belong to a religious institution."[10]

The Unchurched also includes non-believers, although based on the Street Survey experience of which only two people expressed being Atheists, this segment of society is not very large. Through the analysis of the Street Survey responses, both solicited and unsolicited, clear patterns of behavior and beliefs can be discerned regarding these non-participators.

Utilizing the data collected from the Street Survey, it can be surmised that the unchurched are not abandoning the traditional church practices for alternative spirituality activities, which is the contention put forth in *The Spiritual Revolution*.[11] While it is true that fewer people are involved and/or connected with church institutions, the McMinnville Project data suggests that there is no necessary direct connection between disbelief and non-participation. More likely, people are "Believing without Belonging"[12] because they are Sacro-Egoists.

5.1 Unchurched Demographics

To make the Street Survey as appealing and expedient as possible, questions were kept to a minimum and only focused on Sacro-Egoistical elements drawn out of church survey responses. Questions of age, gender, salary, etc. were removed for pragmatic reasons (It was assumed people would be more likely to decline if the survey took over 10-15 minutes to complete). Thus, the complete demographic picture of the unchurched Street Survey participants in McMinnville is still somewhat undefined (besides

---

9. *A Summary of Qualitative Research on the Unchurched*, 7.

10. McCloud, "Liminal Subjectivities and Religious Change," 298.

11. Heelas et al., *The Spiritual Revolution*, 60.

12. See Davie, "Believing Without Belonging," in *Religion in Britain Since 1945*.

their superficially middle class location). However, the Barna Group offers some information on the nationally unchurched demographics.

They state,

> Although they comprise slightly less than half of the national population, men constitute 55% of the unchurched. (2006). The average unchurched person is 41, which is younger than the national norm of 45. (2006). One-fifth of American adults (21%) are single-never-married, whereas nearly one-half of the unchurched fit that definition (48%). (2006)[13]

There is nothing in the Street Survey data to suggest otherwise, demographically. Therefore, this description can be assumed plausible for McMinnville, Oregon as well.

5.2 Sacro-Egoism in Unchurched Society

It would be easy to assume that because some people are not attending church at all; they have no personal stake in spiritual matters in their lives. This is an incorrect assumption. According to the Barna Group, "44% [of the unchurched] claim they have made a personal commitment to Jesus Christ that is still important in their life today (2006)."[14] Shibley states, "To understand religious life in the Pacific Northwest requires thinking outside institutional boxes."[15] Frankiel claims, "The unaffiliated who practice no religion but consider themselves "spiritual" are truly an uncounted force in Pacific-region religious life."[16]

In the Pacific Northwest (normally considered to include the states of Washington, Oregon, and the southwest part of British Columbia, Canada), people "cultivate spiritual lives outside official

---

13. Online: http://www.barna.org/FlexPage.aspx?Page=Topic&TopicID=38.

14. Ibid.

15. Shibley, "Secular But Spiritual in the Pacific Northwest," 164.

16. Frankiel, "The Influence of Alternative Religions," 115.

religious institutions;"[17] however, the modern modus operandi is individualism, not institutionalism, although it is difficult to fully discern what sort of individual religiosity exists outside of the church.

It is possible that there exists a looser, but still poignant relationship between people and their congregation; however, it is harder to define than before in the West. Grace Davie remarks, "The relationships between the community and its church, or churches, are quite as diverse and elusive as those between the two variables, believing and belonging."[18]

Martin's statement that "Although individualism has made inroads into the regularity of religious practice, it mostly stays within the churches as a Christian serve for personal fulfillment,"[19] is not substantiated by the McMinnville Street Survey data. More likely, both the churched and the unchurched have spiritual concerns and interest. Klaas states, "Most pollsters find 70 percent to 80 percent of effectively unchurched people say they have faith or that religion is important to their lives."[20] According to the Barna Group, "More than three out of five (62 percent) unchurched adults consider themselves to be Christian (2006)."[21]

As Doyle notes, "What appears to be new in our time is the notion that an individual's spirituality can be detached from organized religion altogether."[22] It is, therefore, not unexpected that one Street Survey participant added in the unsolicited comments section, "I exercise spirituality by myself in a private manner. I have no need for organized religions." Another person mentioned, "I believe in God, but I am not actively practicing." The volunteer

17. Killen and Shibley, "Secular But Spiritual: Understanding Religious 'Nones';" online: http://www.wkconline.org/index.php/seminar_showcase/ religion_2004_story/understanding_the_nones_those_who_say_they_have _no_religious_affiliation/.

18. Davie, *Religion in Britain Since 1945*, 112.

19. Martin, "Secularisation and the Future of Christianity," 154.

20. Klaas, *In Search of the Unchurched*, 51.

21. Online: http://www.barna.org/FlexPage.aspx?Page=Topic&TopicID =38.

22. Doyle, "Young Catholics & Their Faith," 12.

marked down in her notes that he seemed indifferent to the topic of religion.

Sacro-Egoism markers can be found in the Unchurched section of society, as well as in the Churched, and in parts of the holistic milieu. Sacro-Egoism legitimizes and gives authority to the individual in matters of faith and religion (and perhaps other ethical quandaries). Thus, a person's attitude toward religion and religious institutions is one of the clearest measurements for Sacro-Egoism. However, this disposition does not necessarily mandate a rejection from the unchurched concerning religion/spirituality. Clarke states, "While unchurched spirituality is gaining ground this is not always at the expense of every form of Church-based religion."[23] People can be both "Unchurched" and spiritual at the same time.

Based on the data compiled from the Street Survey, religion and spirituality is not unimportant to the unchurched; only institutionalism is ignored, disregarded, and abandoned. Klaas states, "These people claim faith. They simply choose not to participate in a local community of believers."[24] Based on the McMinnville Project survey results, the "Unchurched" still feel spiritual, but they do not choose to necessarily affiliate themselves with a religion or a denomination.

5.2.1 Attitudes Toward Religion and Church

Street Survey participants who were part of the unchurched segment of McMinnville society frequently expressed an anti-institutional attitude (resulting in non-participation). Bellah states, "Commoner among religious individualist than criticism of religious beliefs is criticism of institutional religion, or the church as such."[25] Kimball adds, "Most people are making conclusions about Christians and Christianity based on a few bad experiences, but

---

23. Clarke, *New Religions in Global Perspective*, 77.

24. Klaas, *In Search of the Unchurched*, 51.

25. Bellah, *Habits of the Heart*, 234.

they are bad enough and reinforced enough to the impression that this is true of all Christians."[26] Hale remarks, "If the Christian gospel is an offense to the unbeliever, it is legitimate to ask whether the central message has in reality been proclaimed and if so whether the offense may lie in the offensiveness of the proclaimers."[27] Klaas summarizes, "In the unchurched society, most unchurched people have separated the miracle of faith from the act of congregational participation."[28] Furthermore, "The popular view of the Church is that it is an institution full of hypocrites."[29]

Often, this anti-institutional mind-set was overtly expressed; however, sometimes it was more inferential in its perception. So, either the unchurched individuals verbalized their discontent with organized religion or they acted upon their condemnation of the church by not attending or caring about its existence. As with some respondents in Andrew Yip's study on sexuality and spirituality (2000), many in the Street survey substantiated by word or deed that "Their reliance on the self in the fashioning of their Christian living has been intensified by church authority, in which they have lost confidence."[30]

On the not-so-subtle side, it was not uncommon to hear remarks during the Street Survey and other contacts with the unchurched along the lines of one survey participant who said he had "Little regard for dictatorial and controlling beliefs." Another participant mentioned that spirituality, to her, was important in "an individual way." Someone else wrote in his or her survey, "Religion is something personal." No one in the Unchurched group ever came out and said, "Gee, I love the Church as a corporate body!" in any way—subtle or blatant.

26. Kimball, *They Like Jesus But Not the Church*, 34.

27. Hale, *The Unchurched*, 185.

28. Klaas, *In Search of the Unchurched*, 4.

29. Hunt, "Understanding the Spirituality of People Who Do Not Go to Church," 164.

30. Yip, "The Self as the Basis of Religious Faith: Spirituality of Gay, Lesbian and Bisexual Christians," 142.

Inferentially, an anti-institutional bent may be perceived when one considers that 85 percent of unchurched in the Street Survey who were not currently attending church had done so in their past. Many had stopped going as teenagers when they were able to assert their independence as young adults. As Hale notes of his own investigation on non-participation, "This study suggests several patterns: early childhood attrition, adolescent disaffection, voluntary or involuntary withdrawal in adulthood as a result of problems of faith or morality; or disengagement in the later years of life."[31] Additionally, 75 percent were not involved in any alternative spirituality practices at any other center or institution. Both traditional and alternative religious or spiritual institutions played a minor role in their lives.

5.2.1.1 RESIDENT REASONS FOR NON-PARTICIPATION IN STREET SURVEY

Many people chose not to participate in the Street Survey, so definitive information on their identification and beliefs is restricted. Wuthnow states, "The deep differences that separate Americans from one another in their views about religious diversity are tempered largely by an implicit strategy of avoidance."[32] However, for reasons already discussed in this chapter, it can be assumed that nearly 80 percent of those who refused to participate in the Street Survey were part of the unchurched milieu in McMinnville —a speculation based on the congregational demographic count showing an attendance rate of 19.8 percent.

Even though they did not overtly share about their personal religious beliefs, the non-participants often provided key information through their excuses. The refusal responses were of three basic types: polite but uninformative responses, those regarding schedule issues, and those regarding religious attitudes.

---

31. Hale, *The Unchurched*, 176.

32. Wuthnow, *America and the Challenges of Religious Diversity*, 229.

A few people politely refused without going into specifics, which the volunteers indicated on the surveys with "No reason given." The volunteers were trained to write down the residents' reasons for non-participation, if possible, and many noted individual responses like, "politely declined" and "not interested" in a few of the cases—this amounted to 20 percent of the total number who refused.

Most of those who refused to take part gave scheduling issues as their reason. The volunteers heard statements such as, "I am doing Karaoke," "We are having a birthday party," "I am on the phone to Germany," "I am in the middle of something," "I am getting lunch ready," "I have the flu," "I am busy cleaning house," "I have no time," "I am busy mowing the lawn," "Everyone is asleep," "I am watching my daughter and watching NASCAR racing," "My grandson is sleeping," "I am painting my house," and "We are going out; there's not enough time." In describing her most humorous survey attempt, one volunteer said, "I said, 'Religion,' he said, 'no.'"

Indirectly, even those choosing not to participate demonstrated or voiced their interest/prioritization of religious matters in their lives. This makes sense if it is as Hale suggests—"Organized religion, they claim, is not relevant to their lives. It does not speak to their individual needs and problems."[33] For many people in the Street Survey, church activities and involvement had a significantly lower priority, for a variety of reasons, than other secular activities in their lives.

All counted, thirteen people declined for scheduling issues—65 percent of the total number who refused to participate. The three remaining people who also refused actually provided religious reasons for their non-participation. One said, "I keep religion to myself"; and the last said, "No," when the volunteer said "Religion." So, "Religion" was officially the reason for their refusals for 15 percent of those not participating in the Street Survey; however, for most, it was simply that they had prioritized other secular events over a survey on Religion.

33. *A Summary of Qualitative Research on the Unchurched*, 16.

5.2.2 Attitudes Toward God/Bible/Prayer

Some of the most provocative data concerned the unchurched' theological positions on several key spiritual issues. As Hunt suggests, "Even those who have deliberately chosen to follow their own spiritual path, and have rejected Christianity, are still in dialogue with the Christian tradition."[34] Seventeen of the twenty (85 percent) indicated that they believed in God. Seventeen of the twenty (85 percent) said that they believed people were basically spiritual. Eighteen of the twenty (90 percent) indicated that they believed in an afterlife. Fourteen of the twenty (70 percent) mentioned they were aware or had been influenced by a spiritual presence in their lives. Two of the fourteen (14 percent) who said they were not attending church, did mention that they still were reading their bibles.

This agrees with numbers collected by Killen and Shibley who state, "While 'Nones' are on the rise, there is no corresponding drop in the percent of the population believing in God or afterlife."[35] Thus, the unchurched are seen to be anti-institutional, but not necessarily atheistic or secular; they are Sacro-Egoistical, which allows for greater spiritual individualism and expression.

As Voas suggests, "A more substantial proportion of the population will privately follow a variety of self-spirituality. Those who are most engaged with the process may reject Christianity, but others will see their spirituality as consistent with Christian identification."[36] Killen and Shibley substantiate this with the statement, "'Nones' are spiritually open even if they don't identify with a religious tradition."[37] Yip remarks, "Some believers might not define themselves as 'religious' in the traditional sense, but this does not mean that a 'spiritual' dimension is absent from

34. Hunt, "Understanding the Spirituality of People Who Do Not Go to Church," 168.

35. Killen and Shibley, "Secular But Spiritual: Understanding Religious 'Nones.'"

36. Voas, "The Rise and Fall of Fuzzy Fidelity in Europe," 13.

37. Killen and Shibley, "Secular But Spiritual: Understanding Religious 'Nones.'"

their lives."[38] Hunt concludes that the unchurched are not "believing without belonging" as Davie suggests, but "It is belief, yes, but not belief in an orthodox Christian God, rather a belief in 'something.'"[39]

Based on the data from the Street Survey, most of the unchurched voiced affirmation for spirituality and religion in their lives. Mostly, this was in the form of traditional activities; no one indicated they were involved in the holistic milieu. Very few people indicated a complete and utter disregard for religion; in fact, the two self-acknowledged Atheists in the Street Survey voiced a strong interest in this project and its results. Based on the Street Survey, the unchurched still take interest in their spiritual and religious lives.

5.2.3 Personal Privacy

One of the most evident characteristics of the unchurched faction in McMinnville is their strong claim on personal privacy. This insistency does not merely revolve around religion, but is also concerned with politics, economics, and even their avocations.

During the door-to-door survey, the volunteers mentioned that occasionally a respondent would reply, "That is none of your business," when asked a specific question from the survey. Another person declined to participate and stated, "Religion is something personal." When one volunteer asked another homeowner if they would be willing to take a survey regarding religion/spirituality, the owner replied, "I keep religion to myself" and quickly closed the door.

Clearly, according to Bellah, for many, "Religion is primarily a private matter having to do with family and local congregation."[40] On this, Clarke remarks, "Speaking generally about the future functions of religion, these will be confined mostly to the private,

38. Yip, "The Self as the Basis of Religious Faith," 135.

39. Hunt, "Understanding the Spirituality of People Who Do Not Go to Church," 164.

40. Bellah, *Habits of the Heart*, 219.

intimate sphere of life."[41] Hunt adds, "As people talk, they share how difficult it is to discuss their own beliefs or spiritual experiences with anyone else. Even raising the issue of religion in general is considered risky."[42]

This active fortification of personal views makes sense in light of Sacro-Egoism, which protects the individual's understanding of their spirituality over outside sources. Thus, sometimes even the innocuous act of being questioned by the McMinnville Project volunteers appeared to be in violation of the "personal safety buffer zones" for many people.

Part of this standoffishness is based on historical precedent; some may be the product of familial or cultural shaming if in variance from normal doctrinal or denominational standards. It is impossible to know with a strong degree of certainty because the participants normally shut down the avenues of exploration before knowledge could be gained.

5.2.4 Apathy and Institutional Inactivity

Another tenet of the unchurched in McMinnville is the reality of inactivity within institutional religion. This is not just a European Exceptionalism facet of religious life. Regarding recent British Social Attitudes surveys and Europe in general, David Voas remarks, "Failure in religious socialization has resulted in whole generations being less active and less believing than the ones that came before."[43]

In another article, Voas adds,

> The dominant attitude towards religion, then, is not one of rejection or hostility. Many of those in the large middle group who are neither religious nor unreligious are willing to identify with a religion, are open to the

41. Clarke, *New Religions in Global Perspective*, 358.

42. Hunt, "Understanding the Spirituality of People Who Do Not Go to Church," 167.

43. Voas and Crockett, "Religion in Britain: Neither Believing Nor Belonging," 20.

existence of God or a higher power, may use the church for rites of passage, and might pray at least occasionally. What seems apparent, though, is that religion plays a very minor role (if any) in their lives.[44]

Anthony King states, "There is little or no evidence of active hostility towards either religious people or religious beliefs. Instead, the national mood appears to be one of benign indifference."[45] This phenomenon can also be observed in Oregon, but a big question concerns whether the appearance of inactivity is equated with apathy or whether there could be another possible reason for its existence. The McMinnville Project evidence suggests that people are not apathetic at all about their spiritual lives.

According to the Street Survey results, it is not that many people do not believe in God or a spiritual side of life; they just do not act upon it in traditional means. Belief is present, but institutional activity was not always a fundamental factor. As one survey-taker put it, "I believe in God, but am not actively practicing. I really am somewhat indifferent to churches."

This is evident when looking at the Street Survey. Of the sixty-five participating households in the Street Survey, forty-one respondents claimed no church affiliation, and forty-five claimed no alternative spiritual activities of any kind. That being said, just because the participants said they were not attending church did not mean they were spiritually or theologically apathetic. When asked, 44.0 percent of respondents said they were participating in other non-church activities such as personal prayer, reading the Bible, youth groups, etc. (See Figure 12). 33.8 percent said they did no outside church spiritual activities, and 30.8 percent did not respond at all.

---

44. Voas, "The Rise and Fall of Fuzzy Fidelity in Europe," 17.

45. King, "Britons' Belief in God Vanishing as Religion is Replaced by Apathy;" online: http://www.telegraph.co.uk/news/main.jhtml?xml=/news/2004/12/27/nfaith27.xml.

	Frequency (Out of 45)	Percent
Awanas, prayer	1	2.2
Bible Study, Softball for Church	1	2.2
Child Evangelism Fellowship; Read Bible	1	2.2
Drug/Alcohol Faith-Based Rehab Program, Prayer, Fasting, Read Bible	1	2.2
High School Youth Groups	1	2.2
Home School Coop, Prayer, Bible Study, Personal Devotions	1	2.2
Mission Trips, Prayer, Bible Reading	1	2.2
Pray and Read Bible	5	11
Prayer	4	8.8
Prayer, Home-School	1	2.2
Reading the Bible	2	4.4
Rotary Club, Masonic Lodge, Habitat For Humanity	1	2.2
Total	20	44.0

Figure 12 - Other Spiritual Activities Outside Church:
Street Survey Results

Therefore, being part of the "Unchurched" does not necessarily indicate a complete rejection of all things religious or spiritual; however, if one is unchurched, then one is more likely to be inactive in institutional religion. According to the Street Survey, these unchurched still perceive themselves as being rather religious or spiritual. These individuals maintain their spirituality or religious connections individualistically without going through mainstream (or holistic milieu) paths.

5.2.5 Spiritual and Secular Prioritization

From the Street Survey, a strong indication of a lowered prioritization of corporate religion and churchgoing is observable. The validity of this aspect of the unchurched in McMinnville is based on the blind approach to the Street Survey, which targeted neither the spiritually minded nor the secularists; it simply focused on a set number of homes in a central location of McMinnville. No religious affiliation or beliefs were foreknown in any of the survey encounters. However, within the entire community of people contacted, three different sub-groups were formed—the participants who were religiously/spiritually active, the participants who were not involved in any spiritual activities, and the non-participating contacts.

All three of these groups offered interesting statements describing their prioritization of religion and spirituality. The volunteers took thorough notes on both the participating and the dissenting residents. The residents' responses to the survey were very enlightening regarding their valuing of spiritual and/or church matters as described earlier.

Even though the Barna Group study suggests that "In a typical week, unchurched people are less likely than other adults to read the Bible or to pray,"[46] for the fifteen in the McMinnville Street Survey who were not involved in a church, this 40 percent of the Street Survey still participated in spiritual activities such as prayer and a Bible study at home, without institutional direction. Furthermore, 73 percent of that group marked that their spiritual life was "pretty" or "very important." They may not be following traditional routes of religiosity in McMinnville, but they still were acting upon their faith in their personal lives.

---

46. "Ratio of 'Unchurched' Up Sharply Since 1991," 15.

5.2.5.1 Atheist Interviews

The same Sacro-Egoistical characteristics can be observed in the responses of the Atheist or non-believer in Oregon to the focus questions. Interviews were arranged for two individuals who espoused to be unattached, uninterested, and unbelieving of the supernatural and/or religion. They were married, in their late thirties, have two children, were middle class, and had lived in Oregon their entire lives.

"Saul" was born in Corvallis, Oregon, forty-five minutes away from McMinnville. He works at a local computer/printer production company as a technical specialist and received collegiate training from West Point Army Academy and Oregon State University. "Deb" was born in Vietnam, but had come over as a young child to Corvallis. She works as a pharmacist at a local super-store and received her education at Oregon State University, too.

Both interviews were done in Corvallis, in their home. The same questions used in other congregational and holistic milieu interviews were presented to the couple. Their responses are listed below with their relevance to Sacro-Egoism.

Both interviewees were asked, "What sort of religious upbringing or experiences do you have?" Deb responded, "My upbringing was laissez-faire. I did go to church and read the Bible, and I wanted to find a place there for me. In the end, I just felt that the church was one big, hypocritical lie and that too much blood had been spilled by and for the 'lambs.'"

Saul responded, "My parents are not religious so I never really cared to explore this very much. When I did consider it more seriously in high school, there were too many illogical things in the Bible to choose to believe in God. That's not to say I don't respect the fact that you believe in God. I just realized that saying I believe in God and actually believing in God are two different things." Clearly, both interviewees have made up their own minds on the matter of religion and choose not to believe or participate for the reasons listed above.

The interviewees were also asked, "What do you think of institutional religion?" Deb responded, "Basically, it sets people up to fail in life and uses the guilt to control them." Saul replied, "I think it's a way to control people. I am not fond of it." When further asked, "What aspect of religious life do you find attractive and why?" Deb remarked, "As a woman, I don't think it is attractive at all." Saul stated, "Not sure exactly what you mean by religious life but if you mean the fellowship with other people of like-minds, I guess that is what is nice about it. However, you don't need religion to get that positive experience."

Regarding their prediction of the religious future in Oregon, when asked, "Where do you see the American Church heading in the future?" Deb answered, "If I was optimistic, I would hope it as well as American society grows up and realizes that other peoples and other ideas exist and are valuable." Saul added, "I don't really care, but I doubt it is leaving our shores anytime soon. I suspect the American Church is here to stay because as long as people want answers to their questions like, 'Why do I exist?,' it will offer things that will reassure people." Despite an implicit cynicism, their responses sounded very similar to Rational Choice Theory.

Being disassociated with traditional religion, one could expect them to embrace other spiritual resources; however, their responses suggest otherwise. When asked, "What do you think of alternative avenues of spirituality, specifically non-traditional Christian ones?" Deb replied, "I don't think it is necessary, but it should not harm anybody either." Saul offered, "I don't think it really matters to me. We actually chose to get married in a Celtic hand-fasting ceremony,[47] which is a bit 'New-Agey,' but we weren't doing it to be spiritual. We just thought it was a good way to express our love and commitment for each other." This shows the Sacro-Egoist characteristic of tolerance for alternative avenues

47. "Handfasting" was the word used by the ancient Celts to describe their traditional trial-marriage ceremony, during which couples were literally bound together. The handfasting was a temporary agreement that expired after a year and a day. However, it could be made permanent after at that time, if both spouses agreed. See "Celtic/Neopagan Handfasting;" online: http://www.religioustolerance.org/mar_hand.htm.

of religiosity without direct beliefs in the holistic milieu spiritual beliefs.

When asked one of the more telling questions regarding Sacro-Egoism—"What has the highest spiritual or religious authority in your life?"—Deb remarked, "The bonds and embrace of family. Ultimately, I want to be responsible for my actions." Saul replied, "I don't have a spiritual or religious authority figure in my life. That's not to say I want one either. My moral compass comes from my own sense of right and wrong."

Both of their responses display a strong indication that for Saul and Deb, they are their own source of authority. In fact, at the end of the conversation, I confided to them that they appeared to both be Sacro-Egoistical, to which Saul responded, "Define 'Sacro-Egoist' for me exactly. If I don't agree with it, I'll find a label for you as well." I told him I wasn't allowed to have a label until after I passed my viva.

Despite their negative responses toward organized religion, there is nothing to suggest any immorality or unethical attitudes in their lives. Deb mentioned, "My parents never pressured me one way or the other, the only thing they insisted on was that I be a good person. I felt I could be a better person without all the fluff in between (like give 10 percent to the church so I could go to heaven, or do *xyz* to be a "good" Christian)." Saul offered, "My parents taught my sister and me to treat others kindly. The Golden Rule prevailed. In the Gulf War, the prospect of dying on the battlefield was scary, but I knew I wasn't going to be a 'foxhole convert.' I respected the other soldiers' choices to consult the chaplain or attend religious services when it was available to them." Both personally chose to "be good" apart from any church instigation or promotion.

Saul and Deb's interviews were quite informative because they demonstrated two facts: 1) they felt absolutely no need for Christianity or the church institute in their daily lives; and 2) their responses clearly showed Sacro-Egoistical characteristics of individual authority, anti-institutionalism, and tolerance for alternative expressions of spirituality. This adds credence to the assertion that Sacro-Egoism is more than just a "religious thing." It is evident in the lives of unbelievers, too. Speaking as a modern Atheist, Lacroix states, "The world is before us; it is always given, but as merely given it is unfulfilled and ambiguous. So it gives itself over to our activity which moulds and achieves it."[48] Therefore, it appears that Sacro-Egoism also touches upon Atheism as well.

5.3 Absence of Holistic Milieu Activities

One of the most profound realities in McMinnville is the great absence (or silence) of the holistic milieu in the lives of the Unchurched. According to recent research, those in this demographic group " . . . also tend to be independent and less involved organizationally—with lower levels of voter registration, less money donated to nonprofit organizations, lower levels of media usage, and less engagement in community service."[49] It is true that there are a few holistic milieu groups that gather, but the traditional religious centers far outweigh the alternative spirituality practice.

The *McMinnville Contemplative Group, Thunders Zen/ Christian, The Baha'i's,* and *The New Thought Group* attendance (combined) is roughly around fifty to seventy-five people (based on emailed information and discussions over the phone with their leaders).[50] This is an incredibly small proportion of McMinnville's population (less than one quarter of 1 percent of McMinnville's population of 29,200), but what if other people, specifically those not associated with a church or denomination, are trying these different alternative spirituality routes but are being overlooked?

The Street Survey took on this task because, if there was a Spiritual Revolution going on within McMinnville, a blind sampling disconnected to the churches or even the holistic milieu

48 Lacroix, *The Meaning of Modern Atheism,* 49.

49. "Ratio of 'Unchurched' Up Sharply Since 1991," 15.

50. Delane, Bahá'í leader, phone interview with author (March 15, 2006); Neil, holistic milieu participant, email message to author (May 26, 2007).

centers would be quite telling. A street survey could show either interaction or avoidance of the holistic milieu outside of traditional or untraditional influence. As Hammond speculates, "Individuals lacking in 'attachments' to others are less inclined toward traditional behaviors like church-going and more inclined toward 'experimental' behaviors."[51] Thus, there should be some evidence in the Street Survey of people engaging in non-traditional spiritual activities; however, the data from the Street Survey in this matter was rather telling.

Not one of the twenty non-churchgoing people indicated that they were doing any of the holistic milieu alternative spirituality practices such as acupuncture, astrology, Buddhism, homeopathy, pagan activities, Reiki, or even Yoga. Based on the McMinnville Project Street Survey results, these people were not abandoning traditional church life and substituting it with holistic milieu activities. In fact, often the activities they indicated they performed away from the church were rather traditional in Christian circles.

In the Street Survey, when asked what alternative spirituality activities they did outside of the church, four people mentioned they prayed, two people mentioned they read the Bible, and two people were involved in elementary or high school Christian faith groups (and none had indicated they attended church). No one mentioned any New Age groups or activities. Moreover, within this same group, when asked if they had felt aware of or were influenced by a spiritual presence, thirteen said they had. They felt aware of this spiritual presence by "small miracles," "bad dreams," "being influenced by a ghost," "speaking in tongues," "when drowning," "birth of my son," and being "in prayer."

Of these responses, none are explicitly taboo in Christian circles nor absent from the stories in the Bible; they were examples one might expect to hear spoken of in a church service.

51. Hammond, "Introduction—Religion in the Pacific Region," 2.

5.4 Conclusions on the Unchurched in McMinnville

The Unchurched demographic group in the city of McMinnville (and in the West as a whole) is, in many ways, an unfamiliar sociological frontier. What and why the Unchurched believe or engage (or not) in religious/spiritual activities remains somewhat cloudy, and more data is needed to help define this significant part of western society in Europe and in the USA. The McMinnville Project and the Kendal Project attempted this endeavor in part, but more investigation needs to occur in the United States and Europe to gain a full picture of the rejection or embrace of religion by those outside of institutional religion. The dilemma will be how to get to this segment of society and how to draw the information from them.

It is easy (yet dangerous) to assume that simply because people are not attending church or officially connected with a belief system that they are unreligious. Speaking of American religiosity, Fuller states, "Despite their [the 40 percent who claim no connection with organized religion] unchurched status, most nonetheless claim to be strongly religious or spiritual on a personal level. Any attempt to understand contemporary American spirituality must therefore look well beyond the boundaries of the nation's churches."[52] Thus, if institutionalism or Sacro-Clericalism is a weak part of modern western society, then something is taking its place.

Based on the McMinnville Project data, Sacro-Egoism is the new religious/spiritual approach of most people today that is replacing Sacro-Clericalism. It gives them the personal power in religious matters they desire, while at the same time proving individualized spiritual nourishment and protection from what they consider to be anachronistic, oppressive, unwanted church rules.

52. Fuller, *Spiritual But Not Religious*, 1.

6

Conclusion

6.0 Introduction

THIS CHAPTER PRESENTS KEY conclusions regarding the research question and hypothesis pursued in the McMinnville Project and the original findings of the McMinnville Project. It then offers several suggestions on potential ways to strengthen the findings and facilitate research on studies such as the McMinnville Project. Finally, it provides explanation on the implications of understanding the contemporary religious milieu utilizing the McMinnville Project data and the idea of Sacro-Egoism and the other Sacro-States.

6.1 Conclusions About Research Hypothesis

The McMinnville Project originally set out to test the Kendal Project's theory of a "Spiritual Revolution" that indicated movement toward the holistic milieu and away from traditional forms of religion.[1] This project provided an excellent snapshot of current religious and spiritual beliefs and activities being undertaken by the citizens in this typical American city with which to compare to Kendal, UK. As with the Kendal Project, church attendees were

1. Heelas et al., *The Spiritual Revolution*, 6-9.

counted, surveys were distributed, and interviews were done, all in order to gain a better understanding of what people were doing in their religious and spiritual lives and for what reasons.

The data collected and analyzed agreed with much that Heelas *et al.* had predicted—a strong sense of individualism, a nurturing of subjective religious preferences and priorities—but it also showed little verification of the Spiritual Revolution contention that the holistic milieu was growing while the traditional religious milieus were waning.[2] In fact, at least superficially, both milieus looked rather anorexic at least in regard to attendance and group participation.

As the survey data was analyzed, however, several patterns began to emerge showing four main groupings of attitudes to religious authority. The strongest perceived pattern indicated the presence in McMinnville society of a strong, individualized commitment to personal spiritual and religious fulfillment alongside of a strongly anti-institutional attitude (Sacro-Egoism).

New Age spirituality was present in the survey data, but was at best negligible in McMinnville society. Survey respondents infrequently indicated participation in an alternative spirituality activity, but also indicated even more infrequently that it had a religious or spiritual dimension to it. The project data patterns also suggested other approaches to religion—mystical, communal, or clerical—with varying intensity and frequent cross-over, but the aforementioned personal commitment attitude was unmistakably evident in the data. These approaches, along with the egoistical approach to religion, are examined in turn below.

6.2 Original Findings

This study has shown that in the city of McMinnville residents express their religiosity in four different ways: Sacro-Egoism, Sacro-Clericalism, Sacro-Theism, and Sacro-Communalism. Each of these Sacro-States approaches religious authority differently.

2. Ibid., 135.

Sacro-Egoism gives ultimate religious and spiritual authority to the self; Sacro-Clericalism gives ultimate authority to the church institution; Sacro-Theism gives ultimate authority to God; and Sacro-Communalism gives ultimate authority to the community of the participant.

Historically, Sacro-Clericalism has been the dominant form for many centuries as is evident in membership numbers; however, based on the survey data compiled in the McMinnville Project (and in other studies), the Sacro-Clericalism presence is not strong in the modern western culture. The religious scene is much different than it was twenty-five years ago, based on the longitudinal information in other sociological studies of the western world.[3]

Whereas once the church institution was favored and highly respected in the community, now it has a poor reputation although it is not completely rejected. Kimball remarks, "The American culture no longer props up the church the way it did, no longer automatically accepts the church as a player at the table in public life, and can be downright hostile to the church's presence."[4]

People are attempting to find personal relevance and reality within the church walls despite their reticence to fully commit. In contemporary McMinnville, Sacro-Egoism represents the strongest expression of faith. This is evident considering the data compiled and analyzed from the churches, holistic milieu, and in the Street Survey in the McMinnville Project, but it can also be observed elsewhere.

The McMinnville Project data suggests that that there is no paradigm shift to the holistic milieu as suggested in *The Spiritual Revolution*;[5] instead, there is an emphasis on religious individualism within church settings. People leave their religious options open to the holistic milieu, but they do not necessarily embrace it, at least spiritually. Secularization is a factor in the local culture,

---

3. "American Religious Identification Survey 2001;" online: http://www.gc.cuny.edu/faculty/research_briefs/aris/aris_part_two.htm.

4. Kimball, *They Like Jesus But Not the Church*, 18.

5. Heelas et al., *The Spiritual Revolution*.

but its effects are not necessarily mortally wounding to religion, based on the data.

Similarly, the Rational Choice Theory has some reverberations in the McMinnville Community, but it, too, does not fully explain the lowered membership and affiliation statistics alongside of the widespread expression of personal, religious faith in this Oregonian city. The religious market, especially relative to church life, should be thriving because of the unfettered religious landscape in Oregon, but it is not, which is a factor that runs counter to Finke and Stark's interpretation of Rational Choice Theory. However, Sacro-Egoism explains this condition through focusing on radical individualism, subjectivism, and autonomism—with an emphasis on the "radicalism" of these sociological aspects. People are still shopping around for their religious needs; however, they currently have new, highly personal, subjective outlets alongside of the traditional offerings.

Essentially, theories that focus on individualization, subjectivization, autonomization, and privatization relate closely to current religious life in McMinnville. Each of these is described further in following sections; however, Sacro-Egoism best explains the dominant expression of faith in McMinnville and gives hints to understanding faith in other parts of the state and country.

The data also supports speculation and investigation regarding those McMinnvillians who embrace the other Sacro-States of Theism, Communalism, and Clericalism. The strongest presence in McMinnville was Sacro-Egoism; however, other Sacro-States' presence was also indicated in the data. Various survey cluster responses were considered in determining the four different approaches to religiosity in McMinnville although three stand out: responses concerning personal/institutional authority, acceptance/rejection of alternative spirituality, and personal/corporate involvement and investment in religious life.

One of the clearest indicators for a Sacro-State revolved around the notion of personal versus institutional authority. Sacro-Clericalism was observable in that only 2.7 percent of the survey respondents in the Congregational study indicated that the church was the highest authority in their life. However, 13.4 percent of the same congregational sample indicated that their own reason, judgment, intuition, or feelings was the highest authority in their lives. Furthermore, 70 percent of respondents indicated that God was their highest authority and yet, in the same sub-sample, or "of this number," only 25.3 percent indicated that God had directly or mystically communicated with them. Therefore, nearly 50 percent of the respondents who said God was their highest authority did not indicate that this was through direct communication. How, then, did God communicate with them? Most likely, they meant through indirect understanding, which means they were their own filters for authority—a Sacro-Egoistical characteristic.

Another indicator revolved around (in)tolerance for alternative avenues of spirituality. Sacro-Clericalism, which resists unregulated religious pursuits, is evidently the approach for 42 percent of respondents who indicated that alternative spirituality forms were unacceptable or unnecessary for Christians. However, 74.7 percent of respondents indicated that alternative spirituality was useful, helpful, or could even teach Christians things—another element of Sacro-Egoism, which allows for experiential religious testing that may benefit the individual on their personal spiritual journey.

Finally, another guide for determining the Sacro-States concerned the prioritization of external or internal religious activity and involvement. Respondents who indicated that they attended church more than once a week (38 percent) could be considered to be Sacro-Clericalists or Sacro-Egoists, although only 2.7 percent of this sub-sample indicated that the church was their highest authority. So, perhaps Sacro-Clericalists only made up 0.07 percent of the respondents attending once a week and the majority, then, were Sacro-Egoists or Sacro-Communalists who were attending for personal gain.

Substantiating this notion further, 27.3 percent of respondents indicated that they had attended another church regularly and had left for personal reasons, which also suggests a Sacro-Egoistical approach to religion because these respondents were shopping around for a religious environment that best served their personal needs.

Besides these three aspects, there is also a tremendous amount of sociological data regarding religion and economics, gender, age, education, etc. that needs to be studied in the future. Thus, not only is there the possibility for still more study in McMinnville, but this project needs to be replicated in other parts of the Pacific Northwest and really in the whole of the United States to help lift the veil over modern personal religiosity.

6.3 Implications for Understanding the Contemporary Religious Milieu

Based on studies such as the Kendal Project,[6] the ARIS study,[7] and the Baylor study,[8] etc., religious life in the western world is changing and the future is uncertain—inviting theoretical speculation on the causes, consequences, and context of religious life. Ellway asks, "Does religious vitality mean primarily the numbers of churchgoers, or numbers of active members only, or does it include those who profess belief when asked but do not participate?"[9]

The McMinnville Project brought to attention the analytical use of Sacro-Egoism and the other Sacro-States in understanding religiosity and personal expression of faith. Sacro-Egoism both confirms and challenges key aspects of Secularization, Rational Choice Theory, and the Individualization of religion. These are considered in turn below.

---

6. *The Kendal Project*; online: http://www.lancs.ac.uk/fss/projects/ieppp/kendal/.

7. "American Religious Identification Survey 2001;" online: http://www.gc.cuny.edu/faculty/research_briefs/aris/aris_part_two.htm.

8. "American Piety in the 21st Century;" online: http://www.baylor.edu/isreligion/index.php?id=40634.

9. Ellway, "Shopping for Faith or Dropping Your Faith?," 10; online: http://www.csa.com/discoveryguides/religion/overview.php.

CONCLUSION

6.3.1 Sacro-Egoism and Secularization Theory

One of the most relevant aspects of Sacro-Egoism regarding religion in the contemporary world concerns participation. Ellway remarks, "It is an open question whether religion, including Christianity, is as terminally ill as ST [Secularization Theory] states."[10] Aldridge adds, "Secularization is often presented as a law of historical development, a universal accompaniment of modernization and an inescapable destiny."[11] That western church membership is declining is incontrovertible; that membership and attendance records are the only way people live out their religiosity is debatable. In fact, the data collected in the McMinnville Project suggests that people exercise their faith both in and out of church settings. The high ratings in the Street Survey data for reading the Bible and praying demonstrate this reality.

Bruce's secularization assumption of religious morbidity that was once considered an irrefutable universal sociological truth has come unto criticism as being unsubstantiated by the presence and resilience of faith in the US and in other non-Western countries in Asia and Latin America.[12] Ellway states, "The USA may be an exception to the general drift in the West towards secularization, if such there be, but it is not the only one."[13]

David Martin remarks,

> If you understand religion as a single and distinct class characterized essentially by empirical mistakes and implausible speculations then you will tend to focus for the most part on how far these have undergone cumulative public discredit. If, however, you understand some religions as sets of apprehensions or sightings or languages expressing alternative logics then you will tend more to trace their modes and mutations.[14]

10. Ibid., 19.

11. Aldridge, *Religion in the Contemporary World*, 87.

12. Jenkins, *The Next Christendom*, 83–85.

13. Ellway, "Shopping for Faith or Dropping Your Faith?," 19.

14. Martin, "On Secularization and its Prediction: A Self-examination," 30.

God still holds a very prominent role in the lives of many people across the globe, despite the presence and resources available in secular Western society.

Furthermore, secularization theory often appears to be self-contradictory depending upon one's interpretation of it. Furseth and Repstad remark, "Secularization may mean that religion becomes more secularly oriented, but also that it withdraws to a 'purer' spiritual-religious sphere."[15] Aldridge adds, "Secularization theorists exaggerate the religiosity of earlier eras, such as the Middle Ages, while seriously underestimating the extent of religious faith today."[16]

This seems to be supported considering the manifestation of radical religious individualism and persistent involvement in American society, but Bruce would disagree. Bruce states, "Privatization, individualism, and relativism are now affecting the US churches in the way they did the British churches in the middle of the twentieth century."[17] This leads him to conclude that if trends continue, the US will be as unchurched as England in the future despite America's different religious culture than in England and Europe.[18]

One problem with Bruce's secularization interpretation is that it assumes that individuals will automatically discard traditional religion as being valueless in an increasingly secular world. Within Bruce's assumptions, the trappings of religion (and Christianity in particular) will always lose out to the resources of modernity. Bruce asserts, "I expect the proportion of people who are largely indifferent to religious ideas to increase and the seriously religious to become a small minority."[19]

It is true that freedom of religion across the Western world permits the individual to make choices for himself/herself that sometimes reside outside of religion. However, the McMinnville

15. Furseth and Repstad, *An Introduction to the Sociology of Religion*, 83.

16. Aldridge, *Religion in the Contemporary World*, 87.

17. Bruce, *God is Dead*, 227.

18. Ibid., 219–228.

19. Ibid., 43.

Project data suggests that people can discard the traditional religious trappings without discarding their personal commitment to spirituality or even church life. If everyone was a Sacro-Clericalist, then Bruce's contention might be correct, but if more people are Sacro-Egoists, as the McMinnville Project data suggests, then it is more about the individual's inner beliefs and less about the church institution's cultural and doctrinal architecture, at least in Oregon. As Voas and Crockett suggest, "Belief in the supernatural is high and reasonably robust while religious practice is substantially lower and has declined more quickly."[20]

In Britain, where a state church has been part of the social landscape for centuries, secularization could seem to be the best interpretation of dwindling religious power in the modern age, but in Oregon, which has never had a state church nor an official religious institution, secularization and low membership numbers may have little in common. To be clear, Sacro-Egoism is not a function of secularization; people are Sacro-Egoistical and are, therefore, finding more relevant and personal ways to express their faith outside of typical church avenues, which leads to a change in church statistics, but not religious fervor.

6.3.2 Sacro-Egoism and the Rational Choice Theory

Another theory that closely shadows Sacro-Egoism is Rational Choice Theory. Furseth and Repstad state, "Rational choice theory argues that individuals turn to religion because they see that it gives them some sort of benefits or rewards."[21]

People in the modern western world start with their own spiritual mind-set, and then they cultivate their personal journeys of religious activity and intensity; people shop around for religious environments that best fit their personal needs and wants. This aspect is evident when one examines the McMinnville Project data and the responses of the participants regarding their religious life.

20. Voas and Crockett, "Religion in Britain: Neither Believing nor Belonging," 12.

21. Furseth and Repstad, *An Introduction to the Sociology of Religion*, 117.

Interviewee Esther remarked, "The problem seems to arise when the institution and structure becomes rigid and does not respond to the needs of the congregation."

Sacro-Egoists are well aware of their needs and the ability (or lack thereof) of religious institutions to meet those needs. They flock to institutions that take care of spiritual wants or they simply give up on institutional religion altogether and try to find assistance on their own. In the congregational survey, 27.3 percent of respondents indicated they had "attended another church in Mc-Minnville regularly." Wuthnow remarks, "Increasing numbers of people . . . are transient and infrequent participants in religious communities."[22] He continues, "Instead of remaining loyal to one congregation, or even depending on where our jobs take us, what happens to be most convenient, and how we happen to feel at the moment"[23] people in the modern world are religiously nomadic.

In other words, they have shopped around before choosing to get involved at the local churches. Not enough relevance, too little connection, and people leave for "greener pastures." Rational Choice theory, therefore, is frequently or chiefly utilized in Sacro-Egoism.

6.3.3 Sacro-Egoism and the Spiritual Revolution

Heelas *et al.'s* description of the "Spiritual Revolution" and Sacro-Egoism are also not necessarily at odds with each other as sociological theories. Sacro-Egoism allows for the individual to choose for themselves avenues of religiosity in the traditional, alternative, or secular sphere. There is a subjective turn to the individual, as Heelas *et al.* suggest, but this turn is not just to the holistic milieu. The holistic milieu is just one aspect of the expression of Sacro-Egoism and Sacro-Communalism by people in McMinnville, Oregon.

---

22. Wuthnow, *Christianity in the 21st Century*, 48.
23. Ibid., 39.

In their introduction, Heelas *et al.* declare, "The expectation would be that in the West those forms of religion that tell their followers to live their lives in conformity with external principles to the neglect of the cultivation of their unique subjective-lives will be in decline."[24] Thus, the institutional church will weaken to the benefit of the holistic milieu groups. It is possible that McMinnvillians could eventually abandon Christianity for the New Age movement, but there is no indication of that in the McMinnville Project data (just the opposite, actually). While it is true that many people dabbled in holistic milieu activities within the congregational study, the vast majority indicated no religious or spiritual value associated with these events.

Also, the Street Survey presented no evidence whatsoever that people had left the church to participate in alternative spirituality practices. Even the holistic milieu participants continued their involvement in mainstream churches despite environments that ran contrary doctrinally to their chosen alternative spirituality attitudes and beliefs.

As with the secularization theory, there is no necessary causal relationship between the Spiritual Revolution trajectories and Sacro-Egoism, in either direction. In fact, the Heelas *et al.* state,

> We have therefore distinguished between two modes or aspects of autonomous personhood: individuated subjectivism, where the strong tendency is to be externally orientated, seeking indirect solutions (material, etc.) to cater for subjective-life, and relational subjectivism, where the tendency is towards concentrating more directly on the exploration of the intricacies of the inner life.[25]

Their explanation seems to complement the definition of Sacro-Egoism in terms of ultimate individual authority and self-direction in spiritual matters. However, if the Spiritual Revolution of Heelas *et al.* is happening in England (and potentially elsewhere in the Western world), Sacro-Egoism is potentially a catalyst.

24. Heelas et al., *The Spiritual Revolution*, 7.
25. Ibid., 97.

The personal, subjective nature of alternative spirituality practices goes hand-in-hand with Sacro-Egoism, which places conventional religious or spiritual control under the authority of the individual in society. Rather than previous institutional or Sacro-Clerical admonishment or condemnation of non-traditional activities, modern western society is more tolerant for personal expression and experimentation specifically encountered in the holistic milieu. The amount of involvement growth in the holistic milieu is in some ways difficult to determine because of its adherents' guarded sense of privacy and due to the current socially fringe nature of alternative spirituality practices.

The manifestation of Sacro-Egoism may be more likely in western communities that uphold personal independence over institutional clout or embrace the benefits of secular society. Whether abandoning or cleaving to traditional church life, more sociological testing needs to be done before coming to any absolute conclusion, but the McMinnville Project (and the Kendal Project) have made steps toward a fuller understanding of the role and importance of the holistic milieu in modern religious life.

6.3.4 Sacro-Egoism and Privatization

Privatization, as with subjectivization and individualization, is another sociological concept that complements Sacro-Egoism in its understanding of the shifting religious power structure in the modern western world. Regarding this change in religious empowerment, Wilson remarks,

> Many of these moral orientations [to dress, forms of speech, eating, courtship, attitudes to strangers, neighbours, kinsmen, etc] were entrenched within a religious view of the world, and both the influence of religious morality and of the religious beliefs which supported them have been largely swept away.[26]

---

26. Wilson, *Religion in Secular Society*, 149.

CONCLUSION

Whereas once the institutions of the church held the reins directing religious life, currently (and especially since the civil rights movements of 1960s), individuals control how much power religion has over and within their lives. Wilson continues, "As the Churches lose the security of acceptance and dominance in communities, and as they reorganize themselves for more central-ized control of their resources, so the character of their operation changes."[27] With this loss of power in society, many scholars (such as Wilson) consider the growing ecumenical, unified voice of Christianity to be only a faltering response to reassert control within society, or at least to stave off elimination.

Beyond diminishing membership numbers, there is clear indication in various sociological studies (Pew Research Center,[28] Kendal Project,[29] McMinnville Project, Yip Project[30]), not to mention in popular culture,[31] that people are disenchanted with the church institute, but not necessarily with religion or spirituality. As Kimball states, "In our post-Christian culture, people encoun-ter a second chasm, the chasm of Christian subculture. We have created this chasm with our rhetoric and attitudes, which have led people today to harbor negative perceptions of Christians and Christianity."[32] People want to exercise their religious freedoms of belief and non-belief free from ecclesiastical edicts, pressure, and judgmentalism, which is a longstanding western attitude.[33]

The presence of Sacro-Egoism within McMinnville society, confirmed by the survey data, affirms this assumption. In the

27. Ibid., 167.

28. "America's Changing Religious Landscape: Christians De-cline Sharply as Share of Population; unaffiliated and Other Faiths Continue to Grow;" online: http://www.pewforum.org/2015/05/12/americas-changing-religious-landscape/.

29. "Methods and Findings;" online: http://www.lancaster.ac.uk/fss/projects/ieppp/kendal/.

30. Yip, "The Self as the Basis of Religious Faith: Spirituality of Gay, Lesbian and Bisexual Christians."

31. Leong, "Dogma Movie Review."

32. Kimball, *They Like Jesus But Not the Church*, 236.

33. Dowley, ed., *Introduction to the History of Christianity*, 436.

McMinnville Project, people repeatedly indicated their require-
ments for religious freedom. Fifty years ago, they had less choice
and the church had more control over them; currently, this is not
the case—individual autonomy reigns. People attend (or not) because of personal choice based on what they can both receive from
and give to the religious communities that they are encountering.

Many churches in the modern world already comprehend
this reality and have begun implementing changes in their worship
life for both survival and success.[34] The church of the future will
need to re-think its activities and goals in an atmosphere that rewards privatization and assumes it to be the status quo. Therefore,
Wuthnow states,

> The challenge before the mainstream is to reclaim those
> earthly realities, to keep their discourses grounded in
> metaphors open to fresh interpretation, and to keep
> spirituality alive through meaningful practices and to
> ward off tendencies toward hardening into rigid forms
> and interpretations.[35]

Sacro-Egoism and religious participation can easily be in operation at the same time. All that is required for the Sacro-Egoist is
that the individual rights, prioritization, and goals are given ample
opportunity to grow and develop, in whatever direction, within
the religious milieu.

Today, in McMinnville, Oregon, people are purposefully and
committedly connecting with the sacred at their deepest personal
levels. As John Stonestreet proclaims, " . . . We're seeing an increase of those who are serious about their faith when it comes to
spiritual disciplines and activities: higher levels of at least weekly
Bible reading, participating in weekly prayer or Bible study groups,
sharing faith with others at least weekly."[36]

34. Kimball, *They Like Jesus But Not the Church*, 16–17.

35. Wuthnow, *Spiritual Marketplace*, 201.

36. Stonestreet, "Americans Becoming Both More, Less Christian;" online: http://www.christianpost.com/news/americans-becoming-both-more-
less-christian-151235/.

A paradigm shift has certainly occurred, and the data suggests movement towards Sacro-Egoism.

6.4 Final Thoughts

In the previous chapters, the purposes, methods, and findings of the McMinnville Project, which set out to replicate the Kendal Project in the US, were presented. Some aspects of the Kendal Project were found to be similar to religious life in McMinnville; however, the McMinnville Project not only negated the notion that traditional authority was slowly being taken over by holistic milieu activities, it also demonstrated that a local (and potentially Western) paradigmatic sociological emphasis of Sacro-Egoism rather than a subjective or secularist turn to alternative spiritualities or non-belief was present. Thus, people in McMinnville are not necessarily caring less about God and/or religion nor are they embracing New Age beliefs; they simply are pursuing individualist methods of expressing their beliefs that are not subject to the authority of churches, ministers, or tradition.

As Flanagan states, "Organised religion has been weakened greatly. Yet, spirituality does not seem to have suffered the same fate. It has become the solace of soul survivors who journey outside organized religion. They find their own uses for spirituality and make their own destinies."[37] However, this individualistic shift away from traditional forms of worship is not moving towards the holistic milieu as is suggested by Heelas et al.;[38] instead, McMinnvillians are actively (but privately) engaging in their spirituality in environs and activities that are more appropriate for the individual.

So, what are citizens of the Pacific Northwest doing in their religious and spiritual life? Past and current data suggests that they are doing what they want to do, which does not necessarily mean going to church or embracing the holistic milieu. In fact, the

---

37. Flanagan and Jupp, eds., *Sociology of Spirituality*, 6.

38. Heelas et al., *The Spiritual Revolution*, 149.

clearest indication is that they are approaching their spirituality with a personal utilitarianism in mind.

According to the survey data, they have not abandoned God or Jesus or the Bible, *per se*, but they are certainly less committed to the church institution or anything that might restrict their religious options. They do what is first best for them, and then for others. Finally, they demand the freedom to worship and live outside the traditional religious "box," and they give others the same courtesy.

Of course, the whole world does not live according to Sacro-Egoism even though it is most easily observed in the West, presently. As alluded to earlier, there are also other "Sacro-State" approaches to religion (Sacro-Theism, Sacro-Clericalism, Sacro-Communalism), both within Christianity and possibly evident in other faiths such as Islam, Hinduism, and Buddhism.

All of these approaches to religion are differentiated in terms of being based on different forms of authority/revelation and are not necessarily sequential or terminal. How much or how intense each one manifests itself in society is still debatable (depending upon the time period and/or cultural context). No one Sacro-State should be considered innately better than another—such valuing is subjective at best and, as mentioned earlier, not what social science is essentially about—discovering the ways people interact with each other in society and the various cultures throughout history.

What can be definitely asserted, currently, is that in Oregon, in the Pacific Northwest, and in the West, Sacro-Egoism is the main approach to religiosity in society—but this has not always been so, nor is it without possibility of change in the future. Everything depends upon the winds of self-regulation or self-promotion in the complex expressions of faith and spirituality, locally and globally.

Afterword

JOHN S. KNOX'S *SACRO-EGOISM: The Rise of Religious Individualism in the West* provides an astute and discerning tool for navigating the present religious cultural milieu. Our current student population at The Biblical Studies Center in Boise, Idaho, has been raised in a confusing and expanding culture without boundaries. This has encouraged young men and women to explore and experiment with every impulse of their hearts, but they have often been left to experience unexpected consequences.

Dallas Willard writes, "Feelings are, with a few exceptions, good servants. But they are disastrous masters,"[1] and young people are beginning to recognize the limitations of an authority that is primarily self-referential—*enter* Sacro-Egoism. However, when one wearies of the ubiquitous salesmanship that accompanies the marketplace of meaning and morality, the first casualty is trust. For contemporary college students, it seems that you're phony until proven authentic, and if you're an evangelical Christian, you're just . . . phony. Therefore, trust must be painstakingly earned, like trying to coax an abused animal to eat out of your hand.

Each week at The Biblical Studies Center, I meet college students who want to learn and grow in their faith, and I see Sacro-egoism in its various forms. One student is enthusiastic, another might be skeptical, still another is proudly apathetic, and all have

---

1. Willard, *Renovation of the Heart: Putting on the Character of Christ*, 122.

been trained by post-modern culture to evaluate their questions and experiences in Sacro-Egoism. With this reality, key questions are raised concerning ministry.

How do we reach and feed the next generation of Christian leaders? Must we simply "leave the food in the dish" and then walk away? How do we minister to those who often want no shepherd? How can pastors and teachers respond to this new paradigm of religiosity?

The answers start with accepting the reality of post-modern American religious society. People approach the faith widely different than they did twenty, fifty, a hundred years ago. Still, after drifting more than a mile off course before landing on D-Day, Theodore Roosevelt, Jr. (the son of President Teddy Roosevelt) famously stated, "We'll begin the war from right here!"[2] Similarly, I would offer the same rallying cry for the ministers seeking to reach the next generation of Christians.

In fact, some of my own ministerial tactics have changed dramatically because of Sacro-Egoism. While I used to put effort into becoming an engaging speaker, I now invest more energy in becoming an engaging listener. Additionally, it is clear the Socratic method[3] has gradually worked its way into a prominent place in my classroom. Attempts to engage in verbal "chess matches" with students have morphed into calmer dialogues that end with an unanswered question or two. Doctrinal mysteries are okay, sometimes. These approaches may aggravate the Sacro-Clerical—the institutional advocates, but they are proving indispensable to reaching Sacro-Egoists, who out number them, currently.

Finally, the insight's provided by Knox's Sacro-State categories need not cause hand-wringing "what-has-the-world-come-to?" laments. In his audio series on apologetics,[4] Alister

2. Ambrose, *D-Day: June 6, 1944—The Climactic Battle of WWII.*

3. "Socrates engaged in questioning of his students in an unending search for truth." Online: http://www.law.uchicago.edu/prospectives/lifeofthemind/socraticmethod.

4. "Why Can We Make Sense of the World;" online: http://www.cslewis-institute.org/audio/by/artist/Alister%20McGrath.

McGrath implores Christians not to try to convert people from postmodernism to modernism before introducing them to Jesus. Instead, he recommends taking them straight to Jesus; the epistemological issues of Sacro-Egoists can get worked out in time and in relationship.

Today's postmodern culture is actually much closer to that of first-century Rome than the modernist after-effects of the Enlightenment. With this in mind, I see Sacro-Egoism not so much as a problem to be solved, but more of a door to greater sociological and pastoral understanding, through which the wise will gladly enter—for the sake of seeing lives transformed in Christ.

Bill Pubols, DMin Candidate

Executive Director
The Biblical Studies Center
Boise, Idaho

Bibliography

A Summary of Qualitative Research on the Unchurched. New York: Religion in American Life, 1979.

"About." *The Biblical Studies Center.* Online: http://www.boisebsc.org/ABOUT. htm.

"About McMinnville." McMinnville Chamber of Commerce. Online: http:// www.mcminnville.org/aboutMcminnville.asp.

Aldridge, Alan. *Religion in the Contemporary World: A Sociological Introduction.* Malden: Blackwell, 2000.

Aldridge, Alan and Ken Levine. *Surveying the Social World: Principles and Practice in Survey Research (Understanding Social Research).* Buckingham: Open University, 2001.

Ambrose, Stephen E. *D-Day: June 6, 1944—The Climactic Battle of WWII.* USA: Simon & Schuster, 1994.

"American Piety in the 21st Century." *Baylor Institute for Studies of Religion,* September 2006. Online: http://www.baylor.edu/isreligion/index. php?id=40634.

"American Religious Identification Survey 2001." *The Graduate Center, CUNY.* Online: http://www.gc.cuny.edu/faculty/research_briefs/aris/aris_part_ two.htm.

"Americans Struggle With Religion's Role at Home and Abroad." *The Pew Forum on Religion & Public Life,* March 20, 2002. Online: http://pewforum.org/ publications/reports/poll2002.pdf.

"America's Changing Religious Landscape: Christians Decline Sharply as Share of Population; Unaffiliated and Other Faiths Continue to Grow." *The Pew Research Center,* May 18, 2015. Online: http://www.pewforum. org/2015/05/12/americas-changing-religious landscape/.

Aston, Nigel. "Decline or Evolution? Religion in Modern Europe." *European History Quarterly* 36/1 (2006) 91–99.

BIBLIOGRAPHY

Aupers, Stef and Dick Houtman. "Beyond the Spiritual Supermarket: The Social and Public Significance of New Age Spirituality." *Journal of Contemporary Religion* 21/2 (May 2006) 201–222.

Bailey, Kenneth D. *Methods of Social Research*. New York: The Free Press, 1994.

Bainbridge, William. *The Sociology of Social Movements*. New York: Routledge, 1997.

Bainbridge, William and Rodney Stark. *The Future of Religion: Secularization, Revival, and Cult Formation*. Berkeley: University of California Press, 1985.

Ballard, Paul. "The Scriptures in Church and Pastoral Practice." *Transformation* 24/1 (January 2007) 34–42.

Barron, Robert. "Not Just Lip Service." *U.S. Catholic* (May 2007) 12–17.

Barton, David. *The Practical Benefit of Christianity*. Aledo: Wallbuilders, 2001.

Beckford, James A. *Social Theory & Religion*. Cambridge: Cambridge University, 2003.

Beckford, James A. and John Walliss, eds. *Theorising Religion: Classical and Contemporary Debates*. Aldershot: Ashgate, 2006.

Bellah, Robert. *Habits of the Heart: Individualism and Commitment in American Life*. Berkeley: University of California, 1985.

Bellah, Robert. "Is There a Common American Culture?" *The Journal for the American Academy of Religion* 66/3 (Fall 1998) 613–625.

———. "New Religious Consciousness: Rejecting the Past, Designing the Future." *The New Republic* (November 23, 1974) 33–41.

Berger, Peter. "The 2000 Paul Hanly Furfey Lecture: Reflections on the Sociology of Religion Today." *Sociology of Religion* 62/4 (2001) 443–454.

———. *The Sacred Canopy: Elements of a Sociological Theory of Religion*. Garden City: Doubleday, 1967.

———. *The Social Reality of Religion: A Treatise in the Sociology of Knowledge*. Middlesex: Penguin, 1967.

Bibby, Reginald W. and Merlin B. Brinkerhoff. "Circulation of the Saints Revisited: A Longitudinal Look at Conservative Church Growth." *Journal for the Scientific Study of Religion* 22/3 (1983) 253–262.

Boorstein, Michelle. "Americans May Be More Religious Than They Realize: Many Without Denomination Have Congregation, Study Finds." *The Washington Post* (September 2006) A12.

Borg, Marcus. *Jesus in Contemporary Scholarship*. Valley Forge: Trinity Press, 1994.

Bruce, Steve. "Christianity in Britain, R.I.P." *Sociology of Religion* 2/2 (Summer 2001) 191–203.

———. *Choice and Religion: A Critique of Rational Choice Theory*. New York: Oxford University, 1999.

———. *God Is Dead*. Massachusetts: Blackwell, 2002.

———. "Praying Alone? Church-Going in Britain and the Putnam Thesis." *Journal of Contemporary Religion* 17/3 (October 2002) 317–328.

BIBLIOGRAPHY

———. *Religion, Modernity, and Postmodernity.* Massachusetts: Blackwell, 1998.

———. "The Demise of Christianity in Britain." In Grace Davie, Paul Heelas, Linda Woodhead, eds. 53–63. *Predicting Religion: Christian, Secular and Alternative Futures.* Aldershot: Ashgate, 2003.

Casanova, Jose. "Beyond European And American Exceptionalisms: Towards a Global Perspective." In Grace Davie, Paul Heelas, Linda Woodhead, eds. 17–29. *Predicting Religion: Christian, Secular and Alternative Futures.* Aldershot: Ashgate, 2003.

"Celtic/Neopagan Handfasting." *ReligiousTolerance.org,* May 31, 2000. Online: http://www.religioustolerance.org/mar_hand.htm.

Chandler, Russell. *Understanding the New Age.* Grand Rapids: Word, 1988.

Clarke, Peter. *New Religions in Global Perspective: Religious Change in the Modern World.* New York: Routledge, 2006.

Corrywright, Dominic. "Network Spirituality: The Schumacher-Resurgence-Kumar Nexus." *Journal of Contemporary Religion* 19/3 (October 2004) 311–327.

Crockett, Alasdair and David Voas. "Generations of Decline: Religious Change in 20th-Century Britain." *Journal for the Scientific Study of Religion* 45/4 (December 2006) 567–584.

Crockett, Clayton. "Post-modernism and its Secrets: Religion Without Religion." *Cross Currents* 52/4 (Winter 2003) 499–515.

Crockett, Clayton, ed. *Secular Theology: American Radical Theological Thought.* New York: Routledge, 2001.

Cross, F. L. and E. A. Livingstone, eds. *The Oxford Dictionary of the Christian Church.* New York: Oxford University Press, 1997.

Crossan, John D. "A Tale of Two Gods." *Christian Century* 110/36 (December 1993) 1270–1278.

Dandelion, Pink. *A Sociology Analysis of the Theology of Quakers: The Silent Revolution.* Lampeter: Edwin Mellen, 1996.

———. *Making Our Connections: The Spirituality of Travel.* Norwich: SCM, 2013.

Davie, Grace. "Praying Alone? Church-going in Britain and Social Capital: A Reply to Steve Bruce." *Journal of Contemporary Religion* 17/3 (October 2002) 329–334.

———. "Event Transcript: Believing Without Belonging: Just How Secular is Europe?" *The Pew Forum on Religion and Public Life,* December 5, 2005; Online: http://pewforum.org/events/index.php?EventID=97.

———. "Prospects for Religion in the Modern World." *The Ecumenical Review* 52/4 (October 2000) 455–464.

———. "Believing Without Belonging: Variations on the Theme." In *Religion in Britain Since 1945.* 93–116. Oxford: Blackwell, 1994.

Davie, Grace and Paul Heelas, Linda Woodhead, eds. *Predicting Religion: Christian, Secular and Alternative Futures.* Aldershot: Ashgate, 2003.

BIBLIOGRAPHY

De Vaus, David, and Ian McAllister. "Gender Differences in Religion." *American Sociological Review* 52 (August 1987) 472–481.

Dobson, James. "Dobson's New Dare." *Christianity Today* 37/8 (February 1993) 69–70.

Doyle, Dennis M. "Young Catholics & Their Faith." *Commonweal* (September 2006) 11–15.

Dowley, Tim, ed. *Introduction to the History of Christianity*. Minneapolis: Fortress, 2002.

Ellway Peter. "Shopping for Faith or Dropping Your Faith?" *CSA Discovery Guides*, May 2005. Online: http://www.csa.com/discoveryguides/religion/overview.php.

Finke, Roger and Rodney Stark. *The Churching of America, 1776–1990: Winners and Losers in our Religious Economy*. New Jersey: Rutgers University Press, 1992.

Flanagan, Kieran and Peter Jupp, eds. *A Sociology of Spirituality*. Aldershot: Ashgate, 2007.

Fletcher, Paul and Hiroko Kawanami, David Smith, Linda Woodhead, eds. *Religions in the Modern World: Traditions and Transformations*. New York: Routledge, 2009.

Flory, Richard and Donald Miller, eds. *Gen X Religion*. New York: Routledge, 2000.

Flory, Richard and Donald Miller. "The Embodied Spirituality of the Post-Boomer Generations." In Kieran Flanagan and Peter Jupp, eds. *A Sociology of Spirituality*. Aldershot: Ashgate, 2007.

Foddy, William. *Constructing Questions for Interviews and Questionnaires: Theory and Practice in Social Research*. Cambridge: Cambridge University Press, 1993.

Focus on the Family. Online: http://resources.family.org/product/id/101899.do.

Fogleman, Lori. "Baylor Survey Finds New Perspectives On U.S. Religious Landscape." *Baylor University Online*, September 2008. Online: http://www.baylor.edu/pr/news.php?action=story&story=52815#.

Fotana, David. *Psychology, Religion, and Spirituality*. Malden: Blackwell, 2003.

Fox, Matthew. "Spirituality for a New Era." In Duncan S. Ferguson, ed. 196–219. *New Age Spirituality: An Assessment*. Louisville: Westminster/John Knox, 1993.

Frankiel, Tamar. "The Influence of Alternative Religions." In Wade Clark Roof and Mark Silk, eds. 109–138. *Religion & Public Life in the Pacific Region: Fluid Identities*. Hartford: AltaMira, 2005.

Fuller, Robert. *Spiritual But Not Religious: Understanding Unchurched America*. New York: Oxford University Press, 2001.

Furseth, Inger and Pål Repstad. *An Introduction to the Sociology of Religion: Classical and Contemporary Perspectives*. Aldershot: Ashgate, 2006.

Gerrish, B. A. *A Prince of the Church: Schleiermacher and the Beginnings of Modern Theology*. Philadelphia: Fortress Press, 1984.

Gibbs, Eddie and Ryan Bolger. *Emerging Churches: Creating Christian Community in Postmodern Cultures.* Great Britain: SPCK, 2006.

Gill, Robin. *Beyond Decline: A Challenge to the Churches.* London: SCM, 1988.

———. *The "Empty" Church Revisited.* Aldershot: Ashgate, 2003.

———. *The Myth of the Empty Church.* Cambridge: SPCK, 1993.

Gilliat-Ray, Sophie. "Civic Religion in England: Traditions and Transformations." *Journal of Contemporary Religion* 14/2 (May 1999) 233–244.

"Godless Hollywood? Bible Belt? New Research Exploring Faith in America's Largest Markets Produces Surprises." *The Barna Group,* August 2005. Online: http://www.barna.org/FlexPage.aspx?Page=BarnaUpdateNarrow&BarnaUpdateID=196.

Golding, Joshua L. *Rationality and Religious Theism.* Aldershot: Ashgate, 2003.

Gonzalez, Justo. *The History of Christianity,* Vol 1 and Vol. 2. San Francisco: HarperSanFrancisco, 1985.

Grasso, Kenneth L. "Christianity, Enlightenment Liberalism, and the Quest for Freedom." *Modern Age* 48/4 (Fall 2006) 301–311.

Greeley, Andrew. "Religious Decline in Europe?" *America: The National Catholic Weekly* 190, no. 7 (March 2004) 16–18.

———. *The Persistence of Religion: Comparative Perspectives on Modern Spiritualities.* London: SCM, 1972.

———. "The Sociology of American Catholics." *Annual Review of Sociology* 5 (1979) 91–111.

Greenfield, Sidney M. and André Droogers. "Syncretic Processes and the Definition of New Religions." *Journal of Contemporary Religion* 18/1 (January 2003) 25–36.

Guest, Mathew and Karin Tusting, Linda Woodhead, eds. *Congregational Studies in the UK: Christianity in a Post-Christian Context.* Aldershot: Ashgate, 2004.

Hadaway, C. Kirk and Penny Long Marler. "How Many Americans Attend Worship Each Week? An Alternative Approach to Measurement." *Journal for the Scientific Study of Religion* 44/3 (September 2005) 307–322.

Hale, J. Russell. *The Unchurched: Who They Are and Why They Stay Away.* San Francisco: Harper & Row, 1977.

Hammett, Edward. *Spiritual Leadership in a Secular Age: Building Bridges Instead of Barriers.* USA: Chalice, 2005.

Hammond, Phillip. "Introduction—Religion in the Pacific Region." In Wade Clark Roof and Mark Silk, eds. 9–20. *Religion & Public Life in the Pacific Region: Fluid Identities.* Hartford: AltaMira, 2005.

———. *Religion and Personal Autonomy: The Third Disestablishment in America.* Columbia: University of South Carolina Press, 1992.

———. "Religion and the Persistence of Identity." *Journal for the Scientific Study of Religion* 27 (1988) 1–11.

Hann, Chris. "Problems with the (De)privatization of Religion." *Anthropology Today* 16/6 (December 2000) 14–20.

BIBLIOGRAPHY

Harris, Sam. *The End of Faith: Religion, Terror, and the Future of Reason.* USA: W. W. Norton, 2005.

Hatcher, Dave. "Saved by Grace V—Election, Free Will, Fairness, and Evangelism." *Trinitykirk.org,* July 21, 2002. Online: http://www.eefweb. org/sermons/topical/Saved%20By%20Grace/Election%20Free%20 Will%20Fairness%20and%20Evangelism.htm.

Heelas, Paul. "The Infirmity Debate: On the Viability of New Age Spiritualities of Life." *Journal of Contemporary Religion* 21/2 (May 2006) 223–240.

———. *The New Age Movement: the Celebration of Self and the Sacralization of Modernity.* Oxford: Blackwell, 1996.

Heelas, Paul and Benjamin Seel. "An Ageing New Age?" In Grace Davie, Paul Heelas, Linda Woodhead, eds. 229–247. *Predicting Religion: Christian, Secular and Alternative Futures.* Aldershot: Ashgate, 2003.

Heelas, Paul and Linda Woodhead, Benjamin Seel, Bronislaw Szerszynski, Karin Tusting, eds. *The Spiritual Revolution: Why Religion is Giving Way to Spirituality.* Malden: Blackwell, 2005.

Henry, Lois Pollard. "Noah's Son—A Parable." *The News-Register* 104/11 (February 7, 1970) 7.

Herzog, A. Regula and Jerald Bachman. "Effects of Questionnaire Length on Response Quality." *Public Opinion Quarterly* 45/4 (Winter 1981) 549–559.

Hoge, Dean R. "Core and Periphery in American Catholic Identity." *Journal of Contemporary Religion* 17/3 (October 2002) 293–301.

Hollinger, Franz. "Does the Counter-Cultural Character of New Age Persist? Investigating Social and Political Attitudes of New Age Followers." *Journal of Contemporary Religion* 19/3 (October 2004) 273–288.

Holland, Tom. "Individualism and the People of God." *Evangel* 23/3 (Autumn 2005) 86–91.

Homan, Roger E. and Pink Dandelion. "The Religious Basis of Resistance and Non-Response: Methodological Note." *Journal of Contemporary Religion* 12/2 (1997) 205–214.

Hunt, Kate. "Understanding the Spirituality of People Who Do Not Go to Church." In Grace Davie, Paul Heelas, Linda Woodhead, eds. 159–169. *Predicting Religion: Christian, Secular and Alternative Futures.* Aldershot: Ashgate, 2003.

Hunt, Stephen. *Religion and Everyday Life (The New Sociology).* New York, NY: Routledge, 2005.

Iannaccone, Laurence. "The Consequences of Religious Market Structure: Adam Smith and the Economics of Religion." *Rationality and Society* 3/2 (April 1991) 156–177.

———. "Rational Choice: Framework for the Scientific Study of Religion." In *Rational Choice Theory and Religion.* Lawrence A. Young, ed. 25–44. New York: Routledge, 1997.

Iannaccone, Laurence and Sean Everton. "Never on Sunny Days: Lessons From Weekly Attendance Counts." *Journal for the Scientific Study of Religion* 43/2 (June 2004) 191–208.

BIBLIOGRAPHY

Jenkins, Philip. *The Next Christendom: The Coming of Global Christianity*. New York: Oxford, 2002.

Karaflogka, Anastasia. "Religion on—Religion in Cyberspace." In Grace Davie, Paul Heelas, Linda Woodhead, eds. 191–202. *Predicting Religion: Christian, Secular and Alternative Futures*. Aldershot: Ashgate, 2003.

Kennedy, Eugene. "Disorganized Religion: The Episcopal and Roman Catholic Church Adopt Different Tactics for Same Problem." *National Catholic Reporter* (January 2007) 20.

Killen, Patricia O'Connell. "Conclusion: Religious Futures in the None Zone." In Patricia O'Connell Killen, Mark Silk, eds. 169–184. *Religion & Public Life in the Pacific Northwest: The None Zone*. Walnut Creek: AltaMira, 2004: 169–184.

Killen, Patricia O'Connell and Mark A. Shibley. "Surveying the Religious Landscape: Historical Trends and Current Patterns in Oregon, Washington, and Alaska." In Patricia O'Connell Killen, Mark Silk, eds. 25–49. *Religion & Public Life in the Pacific Northwest: The None Zone*. Walnut Creek: AltaMira, 2004.

Kimball, Dan. *They Like Jesus But Not the Church: Insights From Emerging Generations*. Grand Rapids: Zondervan, 2007.

King, Anthony. "Britons' Belief in God Vanishing as Religion is Replaced by Apathy." *Telegraph.co.uk*, December 27, 2004. Online: http://www.telegraph.co.uk/news/main.jhtml?xml=/news/2004/12/27/nfaith27.xml.

Klaas, Alan. *In Search of the Unchurched: Why People Don't Join Your Congregation (Once and Future Church Series)*. New York: Alban Institute, 1996.

Knox, John. "Future Emphasis of the Church in the Pacific Northwest." Spring 2014. Online: ChristandCascadia.com.

———. "Radical Individualism in the Modern World." Spring 2014. Online: ChristandCascadia.com.

———. "Sacro-Egoism and the Shifting Paradigm of Religiosity." *Implicit Religion* 11, No. 2 (2008) 153–172.

———. "Sacro-Egoism in Pacific Northwest Blogs." November 2014. Online: http://www.liberty.edu/seminary/index.cfm?PID=26955&ID=777707.

Kosmin, Barry and Seymour P. Lachman. *One Nation Under God: Religion in Contemporary American Society*. New York: Harmony Books, 1993.

Kosmin, Barry A. and Egon Mayer, Ariela Keysar. *American Religious Identification Survey: 2001 (The Graduate Center of the City University of New York)*. Online: http://www.gc.cuny.edu/faculty/research_briefs/aris/aris_index.htm.

Kreider, Alan. "Beyond Bosch: The Early Church and the Christendom Shift." *International Bulletin of Missionary Research* 29/2 (April 2005) 59–68.

Lacroix, Jean. *The Meaning of Modern Atheism*. Garret Barden trans. Dublin: Gill & Son, 1965.

Laird, Lance. "Religions of the Pacific Rim in the Pacific Northwest." In Patricia O'Connell Killen, Mark Silk, eds. 107–137. *Religion & Public Life in the Pacific Northwest: The None Zone.* Walnut Creek: AltaMira, 2004.

Lambert, Yves. "A Turning Point in Religious Evolution in Europe." *Journal of Contemporary Religion* 19/1 (2004) 29–45.

Larsen, Bob. *Straight Answers on the New Age.* Nashville: Thomas Nelson, 1989.

Lataster, Raphael. "New Theologians, New Atheists, and Public Engagement." *Alternative Spirituality and Religion Review* 4/1 (2013) 70–91.

Layne, Ben H. and Dennis N. Thompson. "Questionnaire Page Length and Return Rate." *The Journal of Social Psychology* 113 (April 1981) 291–292.

Leong, Anthony. "Dogma Movie Review." *Media Circus*, 1999. Online: http://www.mediacircus.net/dogma.html.

Liebman, Charles. "Extremism as a Religious Norm." *Journal for the Scientific Study of Religion* 22/1 (March 1983) 75–86.

Lockery, David, ed. *The Challenge of Postmodernism: An Evangelical Engagement.* Grand Rapids: Baker Academic, 2001.

Lucas, Philip Charles and Thomas Robbins, eds. *New Religious Movements in the 21st Century: Legal, Political, and Social Challenges in Global Perspective.* New York: Routledge, 2004.

Luckman, Thomas. "The Privatisation of Religion and Morality." In Paul Heelas, Scott Lash, and Paul Morris, eds. 72–86. *Detraditionalization: Critical Reflections on Authority and Identity.* Oxford: Blackwell, 1996.

Lynch, Gordon. *The New Spirituality: An Introduction to Progressive Belief in the Twenty-First Century.* London: I.B. Tauris, 2007.

Lyon, David. *Jesus in Disneyland: Religion in Postmodern Times.* Malden: Blackwell, 2000.

Macquarrie, John. *Twentieth-Century Religious Thought.* London: SCM, 1988.

Martin, David. *On Secularization: Towards a Revised General Theory.* Aldershot: Ashgate, 2005.

———. "On Secularization and its Prediction: A Self-examination." In Grace Davie, Paul Heelas, Linda Woodhead, eds. 30–39. *Predicting Religion: Christian, Secular and Alternative Futures.* Aldershot, UK: Ashgate, 2003.

———. "Secularisation and the Future of Christianity." *Journal of Contemporary Religion* 20/2 (2005) 145–160.

Matthews, Roy and F. DeWitt Platt. *The Western Humanities.* New York: McGraw-Hill, 2004.

McCloud, Sean. "Liminal Subjectivities and Religious Change: Circumscribing Giddens for the Study of Contemporary American Religion." *Journal of Contemporary Religion* 22/3 (October 2007) 295–309.

McCracken, Brett. *Hipster Christianity: When Church and Cool Collide.* Grand Rapids: Baker, 2010.

———. "Hipster Faith: To Remain Relevant, Many Evangelical Pastors Are Following the Lead of Hipster Trendsetters. So What Happens When 'Cool' Meets Christ?" *Christianity Today (Online)*, September 3, 2010.

Online: http://www.christianitytoday.com/ct/2010/september/9.24.html? start=2.

McGavran, Donald. *Understanding Church Growth*. Grand Rapids, Michigan: Eerdmans, 1970.

McGrath, Alister E. *An Introduction to Christianity*. Malden: Blackwell, 1997.

————. *Historical Theology: An Introduction to the History of Christian Thought*. Malden: Blackwell, 1998.

————. "Why Can We Make Sense of the World." *C.S. Lewis Institute*, 2003. Online: http://www.cslewisinstitute.org/audio/by/artist/Alister%20 McGrath

McKay, John P. and Bennett D. Hill, John Buckler. *A History of Western Society*. USA: Houghton Mifflin, 2006.

McKnight, Scot. "Five Streams of the Emerging Church." *Christianity Today* 51/2 (February 2007) 34–39.

"McMinnville & Amity Yellow Pages." *General Telephone Company of the Northwest*, October 1970.

Melton, J. Gordon. "The Fate of NRMs and Their Detractors in Twenty-First Century America." Phillip Charles Lucas, Thomas Robbins, eds. 229–240. *New Religious Movements in the 21st Century: Legal, Political, and Social Challenges in Global Perspective*. Great Britain, Routledge, 2004.

Milbank, John, *Theology & Social Theory: Beyond Secular Reason*. Malden: Blackwell, 2006.

Miller, Donald. *Blue Like Jazz: Nonreligious Thoughts on Christian Spirituality*. Nashville: Thomas Nelson, 2003.

Minerd, Jeff. "The New Individualism." *The Futurist* 32/9 (December 1998) 1.

Mirus, Jeff. "Religious Privatization and the Need for Community." *Catholic Culture: Living the Catholic Life (Online)*, June 14, 2005. Online: http:// www.catholicculture.org/commentary/articles.cfm?id=64.

Miyakawa, T. Scott. *Protestants and Pioneers: Individualism, and Conformity on the American Frontier*. Chicago: University of Chicago Press, 1964.

Modern, John Lardas. "Ghosts of Sing Sing, or the Metaphysics of Secularism." *Journal of the American Academy of Religion* 75/3 (September 2007) 615–650.

Molloy, Michael. *Experiencing the World's Religions: Tradition, Challenge, and Change*. USA: Mayfield, 2002.

"Mysticism." *New Advent: Catholic Encyclopedia*. Online: http://www. newadvent.org/cathen/10663b.htm.

Newbigin, Lesslie. *Foolishness to the Greeks: The Gospel and Western Culture*. Grand Rapids: Wm. B Eerdmans, 1986.

Newport, John. *The New Age Movement and the Biblical Worldview: Conflict and Dialogue*. Grand Rapids: Wm. B. Eerdmans, 1998.

O'Connell Killen, Mark Silk, eds. 51–77. *Religion & Public Life in the Pacific Northwest: The None Zone*. Walnut Creek: AltaMira, 2004.

O'Dea, Thomas. "Five Dilemmas in the Institutionalization of Religion." *Journal for the Scientific Study of Religion* 1/1 (October 1961) 30–41.

Olds, Glenn A. "The New Age: Historical and Metaphysical Foundations." In Duncan S. Ferguson, ed. *New Age Spirituality: An Assessment*. Kentucky: Westminster/John Knox, 1993.

Olson, Daniel V. A. "Religious Pluralism and US Church Membership: A Reassessment." *Sociology of Religion* 60/2 (Summer 1999) 149–173.

Olson, David T. *The American Church in Crisis: Groundbreaking Research Based on a National Database of Over 200,000 Churches*. Grand Rapids: Zondervan, 2008.

Olson, Roger E. *The Story of Christian Theology: Twenty Centuries of Tradition & Reform*. Illinois: InterVarsity, 1999.

"Oregon." *Hometownusa.com*. Online: http://www.hometownusa.com/or/.

Pacwa, Father Mitch. *Catholics and the New Age: How Good People Are Being Drawn Into Jungian Psychology, the Enneagram and the New Age of Aquarius*. Ann Arbor: Servant, 1992.

"Paris Hilton: God Has Given Me This New Chance." *Foxnews.com*, June 11, 2005. Online: http://www.foxnews.com/story/0,2933,280415,00.html.

Partridge, Christopher. *The Re-Enchantment of the West: Volume 2*. Great Britain: T&T Clark, 2005.

———. "Truth, Authority, and Epistemological Individualism in New Age Thought." *Journal of Contemporary Religion* 14, no. 1 (January 1999) 77–96.

Pasek, Zbigniew, "Man and Nature—A New Project on New Spirituality." *Problems of Sustainable Development* 7/2 (June 2012) 67–76.

Percy, Martyn. "A Place at High Table? Assessing the Future of Charismatic Christianity." In Grace Davie, Paul Heelas, Linda Woodhead, eds. 95–108. *Predicting Religion: Christian, Secular and Alternative Futures*. Aldershot: Ashgate, 2003.

———. *The Salt of the Earth: Religious Resilience in a Secular Age*. London: Sheffield, 2001.

Peters, George. *A Theology of Church Growth (Contemporary Evangelical Perspectives)*. Grand Rapids: Zondervan, 1981.

"PhoneBook: Residential Edition for Yamhill County, 1985." *Greater McMinnville Chamber of Commerce*, 1985.

Pontifical Councils for Culture and Interreligious Dialogue: Section 6.2. Online: http://www.vatican.va/roman_curia/pontifical_councils/interelg/documents/rc_pc_intere   g_doc_20030203_new-age_en.html#6.2.%20 Practical%20steps.

Putnam, Robert. *Bowling Alone: The Collapse and Revival of American Community*. New York: Simon & Schuster, 2000.

Radford, Tim. "Study Refutes Faith in Silent Majority." *The Guardian* (August 16, 2005). Online: http://www.theguardian.com/science/2005/aug/16/religion.news.

"Ratio of 'Unchurched' Up Sharply Since 1991." *Christian Century* 121/11 (June 1, 2004) 15.

BIBLIOGRAPHY

Reeves, Thomas. *The Empty Church: The Suicide of Liberal Christianity.* New York: Free Press, 1996.

Regele, Mike. *Death of the Church.* Grand Rapids: Zondervan, 1995.

"Religious Activity Increasing in the West." *The Barna Group: The Barna Update,* March 1, 2004. Online: http://www.barna.org/FlexPage.aspx?Page=BarnaUpdate&BarnaUpdateID=159.

Religious Tolerance. Online: http://www.religioustolerance.org/newage.htm.

Richardson, Alan. *History Sacred and Profane: Bampton Lectures for 1962.* London: SCM, 1964.

Robinson, Richard. *An Atheist's Values.* Oxford: Blackwell, 1975.

Roof, Wade Clark. "God is in the Details: Reflections on Religion's Public Presence in the United States in the Mid-1990s." *Sociology of Religion* 57/2 (1996) 148–162.

———. *Religion & Public Life in the Pacific Region: Fluid Identities.* Lanham: AltaMira, 2005.

———. "Religion In The Pacific Region: Demographic Patterns." In Wade Clark Roof and Mark Silk, eds. 25–56. *Religion & Public Life in the Pacific Region: Fluid Identities.* Hartford: AltaMira, 2005.

———. *Spiritual Marketplace: Baby Boomers and the Remaking of American Religion.* Princeton: Princeton University, 1999.

Rose, Stuart. "Is the Term 'Spirituality' a Word that Everyone Uses But Nobody Knows What Anyone Means by it?" *Journal of Contemporary Religion* 16/2 (May 2001) 193–207.

Saad, Lydia. "Americans Believe Religion is Losing Clout." *Gallup.com.* Online: http://www.gallup.com/poll/113533/Americans-Believe-Religion-Losing-Clout.aspx.

Salganik, Matthew and D.D. Heckathorn. "Sampling and Estimation in Hidden Populations Using Respondent-Driven Sampling." *Sociological Methodology* 34/1 (2004) 193–239.

Sawyer, Mary. *The Church on the Margins: Living Christian Community.* New York: Trinity, 2003.

Shaffir, William B. and Robert A. Stebbins. *Experiencing Fieldwork: An Inside View of Qualitative Research.* Newbury Park: Sage, 1991.

Shibley, Mark. "Secular but Spiritual in the Pacific Northwest' Zone." In Patricia O'Connell Killen, Mark Silk, eds. 139–167. *Religion & Public Life in the Pacific Northwest: The None Zone.* Walnut Creek: AltaMira, 2004.

Smith, Alex G. *Buddhism Through Christian Eyes.* Littleton: Overseas Missionary Fellowship, 2001.

Smith, Christian. *Going to the Root: Nine Proposals for Radical Church Renewal.* Scottdale: Herald, 1992.

———. "Why Christianity Works." *Sociology of Religion* 68/2 (Summer 2007) 165–178.

Smith, Christian and Melinda Lundquist Denton. *Soul Searching: The Religious and Spiritual Lives of American Teenagers.* New York: Oxford University Press, 2005.

BIBLIOGRAPHY

Soden, Dale. "Contesting for the Soul of an Unlikely Land: Mainline Protestants, Catholics, and Reform and Conservative Jews in the Pacific Northwest' Zone." In Patricia

Stark, Rodney. "Atheism, Faith, and the Social Scientific Study of Religion." *Journal of Contemporary Religion* 13/2 (May 1998) 41–62.

———. "Secularization: The Myth of Religious Decline." *Fides et Historia* 30/2 (Summer/Fall 1998) 1–19.

———. "The Rise and Fall of Christian Science." *Journal of Contemporary Religion* 13/2 (May 1998) 189–214.

Stark, Rodney and Laurence Iannaccone. "A Supply-Side Reinterpretation of the 'Secularization' of Europe." *Journal for the Scientific Study of Religion* 33/3 (September 1994) 230–252.

Starks, Brian and Robert Robinson. "Moral Cosmology, Religion, and Adult Values for Children." *Journal for the Scientific Study of Religion* 46/1 (March 2007) 17–35.

Stonestreet, John. "Americans Becoming Both More, Less Christian." *CP Opinion*, December 15, 2015. Online: http://www.christianpost.com/news/americans-becoming-both-more less-christian-151235/.

"Street Survey Findings." *The Kendal Project*. Online: http://www.lancs.ac.uk/fss/projects/ieppp/kendal/streetsurveyfindings.htm.

Sutherland, Elisabeth. "Quakers and Spiritual Direction." Master's Thesis, University of Birmingham, 2012.

Swatos, Jr., William, ed. "Rational Choice Theory." 402–404. In *Encyclopedia of Religion and Society*. AltaMira, 1998.

Szerszynski, Bronislaw. "Rethinking the Secular: Science, Technology, and Religion Today." *Zygon* 40/4 (December 2005) 813–822.

Tamney, Joseph B. "Does Strictness Explain the Appeal of Working-Class Conservative Protestant Congregations?" *Sociology of Religion* 66/3 (Fall 2005) 283–302.

———. *The Resilience of Conservative Religion: The Case of Popular, Conservative Protestant Congregations*. Cambridge: Cambridge University Press, 2002.

Tamney, Joseph B. and Stephen D. Johnson. "Religious Diversity and Ecumenical Social Action." *Review of Religious Research* 32/1 (September 1990) 16–26.

———. "The Popularity of Strict Churches." *Review of Religious Research* 39/3 (March 1998) 209–223.

Tamney, Joseph B. and Shawn Powell, and Stephan Johnson. "Innovation Theory and Religious Nones." *Journal for the Scientific Study of Religion* 28/2 (1989) 216–229.

Taylor, Charles. "Religious Mobilizations." *Public Culture* 18/2 (Spring 2006) 281–300.

———. "Risking Belief: Why William James Still Matters." *Commonweal* 129/5 (March 8, 2002) 14–17.

———. *Varieties of Religion Today: William James Revisited*. Cambridge: Harvard University Press, 2002.

BIBLIOGRAPHY

"The 2000 Census." *United States Census Bureau.* Online: http://quickfacts. census.gov/qfd/.

"The Socratic Method." The University of Chicago: The Law School. Online: http://www.law.uchicago.edu/prospectives/lifeofthemind/socratic method.

The Unchurched American . . . 10 Years Later. Princeton: Princeton Religion Research Center, 1988.

Traver, Sheldon and John Fortmeyer. "Just How Spiritually Healthy is the Pacific Northwest?" *Christian News Northwest* 11/8 (January 2005) 1.

Voas, David. "The Rise and Fall of Fuzzy Fidelity in Europe." *European Sociology Review* 25/2 (2009) 155–168.

Voas, David and Alasdair Crockett. "Religion in Britain: Neither Believing nor Belonging." *Sociology* 39/1 (2005) 11–28.

Wacker, Grant. "A Tar Heel Perspective on The Third Disestablishment." *Journal for the Scientific Study of Religion* 30/4 (1991) 519–525.

Wallis, Roy and Steve Bruce. "Religion: The British Contribution." *The British Journal of Sociology* 40/3 (September 1989) 493–520.

Wallis, Roy and Steve Bruce. "Secularization: Trends, Data, and Theory." *Research in the Social Scientific Study of Religion* 3 (1991) 1–31.

"Weather." *Travelportland.com.* Online: http://www.travelportland.com/ visitors/weather.html.

Weber, Max. *The Sociology of Religion.* Boston: Beacon Press, 1964/1922.

Wellman, Jr., James. "The Churching of the Pacific Northwest: The Rise of Sectarian Entrepreneurs." In Patricia O'Connell Killen, Mark Silk, eds. 79–105. *Religion & Public Life in the Pacific Northwest: The None Zone.* Walnut Creek: AltaMira, 2004.

Wetzstein, Cheryl. "Christians on the Retreat in the US as the Number of Unchurched Surge." *The Washington Times,* May 12, 2015. Online: http://www.washingtontimes.com/news/2015/may/12/americans-less-christian-more unaffiliated-survey-/?page=all.

Whitemarsh, Darylann and Bill Reisman. *Subtle Serpent: New Age in the Classroom.* USA: Huntington House, 1992.

Willard, Dallas. *Renovation of the Heart: Putting on the Character of Christ.* Colorado Springs: Navpress, 2011. Kindle Edition.

Wilson, Bryan. "Prediction and Prophecy in the Future of Religion." In Grace Davie, Paul Heelas, Linda Woodhead, eds. 64–73. *Predicting Religion: Christian, Secular and Alternative Futures.* Aldershot: Ashgate, 2003.

———. *Religion in Sociological Perspective.* New York: Oxford University, 1982.

———. *Religion in Secular Society.* London: C.A. Watts, 1966.

———. "The Return of the Sacred." *Journal for the Scientific Study of Religion* 18/3 (September 1979) 268–280.

———. *The Social Dimensions of Sectarianism: Sects and New Religious Movements in Contemporary Society.* New York: Oxford University, 1990.

Woodhead, Linda, ed. *Peter Berger and the Study of Religion.* London: Routledge, 2001.

BIBLIOGRAPHY

———. *Christianity: A Very Short Introduction.* Oxford: Oxford University, 2004.

———. "Studying Religion and Modernity." In Linda Woodhead, Paul Fletcher, Hiroko Kawanami, David Smith, eds. 1–15. *Religions in the Modern World.* London: Routledge, 2002.

Woodhead, Linda and Paul Heelas, Grace Davie. "Introduction—On the Importance of Looking to the Future: Prophets and Predictions." In Grace Davie, Paul Heelas, Linda Woodhead, eds. 1–14. *Predicting Religion: Christian, Secular and Alternative Futures.* Aldershot: Ashgate, 2003.

Wuthnow, Robert. *America and the Challenges of Religious Diversity.* Princeton: Princeton University, 2005.

———. *Christianity in the Twenty-first Century: Reflections on the Challenges Ahead.* New York: Oxford University, 1993.

———. *Spiritual Marketplace: Baby Boomers and the Remaking of American Religion.* Princeton: Princeton University, 1999.

———. "The Consciousness Reformation." *Journal for the Scientific Study of Religion* 16/3 (September 1977) 328–329.

YellowBook (2007–2008): Greater Yamhill County. USA: Yellow Book, 2007.

Yip, Andrew. "The Self as the Basis of Religious Faith: Spirituality of Gay, Lesbian and Bisexual Christians." In Grace Davie, Paul Heelas, Linda Woodhead, eds. 135–146. *Predicting Religion: Christian, Secular and Alternative Futures.* Aldershot: Ashgate, 2003.

Young, Lawrence A., ed. *Rational Choice Theory and Religion: Summary and Assessment.* New York: Routledge, 1997.

York, Michael. "New Age Commodification and Appropriation of Spirituality." *Journal of Contemporary Religion* 16/3 (October 2001) 361–372.

Zohar, Danah and Ian Marshall. *Spiritual Intelligence: The Ultimate Intelligence.* Great Britain: Bloomsburg, 2000.

Subject Index

Index of People

INDEX OF PEOPLE